INTRODUCTION

THE HISTORY OF UKRAINE is one of continuous struggle for independence and the right to exist. In 1991, this dream, nursed for centuries, finally became reality. Today, Ukraine is politically independent, an equal member of the world's commonwealth of states, and doing its best to build a democratic society.

Despite severe economic difficulties, natural for any country in the midst of a transfer from a socialist command to a free-market economy, Ukrainians are optomistic that the changes are irreversible.

As one of the largest countries in Europe, in terms of area and population, with some of the most fertile soil in the world, and the hard-working and peace-loving nature of its people, Ukraine will undoubtedly become one of the most prosperous countries of the 21st century.

CONTENTS

Looking after baby brother.

3   INTRODUCTION

7   GEOGRAPHY
     *Geographical regions • Rivers • Climate • Fauna
     • Administrative divisions • Cities*

15   HISTORY
     *The earliest days • Kyivan Rus • Struggle for power, defence
     against invaders • 17th century Ukraine • Ukraine in the Russian
     Empire • Soviet power in Ukraine • Integration of Ukraine into
     the Soviet Union • World War II • Modern Ukraine*

27   GOVERNMENT
     *Legislation • Federal government • Executive power • Law and
     order • The military • Local government*

35   ECONOMY
     *State versus private • Far abroad and near abroad
     • Unemployment • Transportation • Manufacturing
     • Agriculture • Collective, state, and private farming • Energy*

45   UKRAINIANS
     *Minorities • The Tatars • National features • National dress
     • Ukrainian names • Famous Ukrainians*

57   LIFESTYLE
     *A house or an apartment? • Backyard farming • Ukrainian
     women • Life cycle • Education • Medicine • Social services
     • Communication • Employment • Moving around*

71   RELIGION
     *History of Christianity • Christian architecture • What is
     Orthodox? • Other religious denominations • Religion today*

CONTENTS

79 LANGUAGE
Ukrainian • Written Ukrainian • The mass media in Ukraine • Dialects and non-verbal communication • Forms of address • Tatar

89 ARTS
Religious icons • Embroidery • Pottery • Easter eggs • Music • Dance • Literature, film, and theater

97 LEISURE
At home • Television and newspapers • Sports • Travel • Alone with nature

105 FESTIVALS
Remembering the war • International Women's Day • Christmas • Easter • New Year • Other holidays

113 FOOD
Fruits and vegetables • National cuisine • Drinks • Entertaining at home • Alcohol • Eating out

122 MAP OF UKRAINE

124 QUICK NOTES

125 GLOSSARY

126 BIBLIOGRAPHY

126 INDEX

Hanging the clothes to dry in the warm autumn sun.

CULTURES OF THE WORLD

UKRAINE

Volodymyr Bassis

TIMES BOOKS INTERNATIONAL
Singapore • Kuala Lumpur

Cultures of the World
Editorial Director   Shirley Hew
Managing Editor   Shova Loh
Editors   Elizabeth Berg
    Harlinah Whyte
    Tan Jin Hock
    Susan McKay
    Falaq Kagda
Picture Editor   Susan Jane Manuel
Production   Anthoney Chua
Design   Tuck Loong
    Jailani Basari
    Hasnah Mohamed Esa
    Loo Chuan Ming

Originated and designed by
Times Books International,
an imprint of Times Editions Pte Ltd
Times Centre, 1 New Industrial Road
Singapore 536196
Tel: 2848844 Fax: 2854871
Email: te@corp.tpl.com.sg

© Times Editions Pte Ltd 1997

Printed by Welpac Printing & Packaging Pte Ltd

ISBN 981 204 719 0

GEOGRAPHY

PRIOR TO 1991, Ukraine was part of the Union of Soviet Socialist Republics (USSR). Today, it is an independent state located in southeastern Europe. Ukraine is 233,100 square miles (603,730 square km), making it the largest country located completely in Europe. France is only slightly smaller, and the state of Texas only slightly larger. To the north, Ukraine borders Belarus; to the northeast, Russia. Turkey and Bulgaria are located just across the Black Sea in the south, while Romania, Moldova, Hungary, Slovakia, and Poland lie to the west and southwest.

Ukraine's geographical position brought the country under the influence of many different cultures and civilizations. Once the country was freed from foreign rule, Ukrainians were able to make use of the remarkable natural resources of climate, minerals, and soil.

Opposite: **The Privdennyy Bug River winds through central Ukraine.**

Left: **Countryside around the village of Verhna near Lviv.**

7

In southwestern Ukraine, the foothills slowly rise until they meet the Carpathian Mountains.

GEOGRAPHICAL REGIONS

There are no domestic borders on the administrative map of Ukraine indicating the end of eastern Ukraine and the beginning of western. However, Ukrainians distinguish between central, eastern, southern, western Ukraine, and the Crimea. Geographically, Ukraine is divided into two major regions by a line running from the southwest of the country to the northeast. The line crosses the Dnipro River approximately halfway between Kyiv and Dnipropetrovsk.

The southern zone is drier with a more continental climate and steppe vegetation. The northern zone is characterized by deciduous or mixed forest vegetation and experiences a moister and cooler climate.

Approximately 55% of all land in Ukraine is cultivated and more than 70% is used for general agricultural purposes. During the last glacial period, the entire country was covered with a layer of loess, which forms the basis of the thick, black, fertile soil throughout the country.

RIVERS

Several rivers carve their paths through the Carpathian Mountains in the west, including the Tysa, the Cheremosh, the Stryy, and the Dnister. The Dnister is one of the fastest flowing rivers in Europe, running for 876 miles (1,409 km) almost entirely in Ukraine before it empties into the Black Sea. The Dnipro follows nearly the same route in the east. It is the largest river in Ukraine, running south from its source in Russia for 1,420 miles (2,285 km) until it reaches the Black Sea, which it enters near the city of Kherson. The Dnipro is to Ukraine what the Nile and Amazon are to Egypt and Brazil. It is an important passenger, tourist, and cargo way. The main tributaries are Pryp'yat and Desna. The Danube runs along the southwestern border, separating Ukraine from Romania. The Privdennyy Bug is the large river that runs through central Ukraine.

Sunflowers are one of the primary crops grown in Ukraine. Sunflowers are very valuable because the leaves are used for fodder, the flowers for dye, and the seeds for cooking oil.

CLIMATE

Ukraine's comparatively even landscape and gradual temperature changes prevent tornadoes, hurricanes, and other weather extremes. Ukraine has a moderate continental climate with four distinct seasons.

In northern Ukraine, cooler weather with temperatures around 30°F (-1°C) and occasional snow may begin as early as the middle of October, and last right into the month of March. Relief plays an important role in the Carpathian and Crimean Mountains, lowering temperatures and increasing precipitation, while in the coastal areas, the waters of the Black Sea and Sea of Azov cause a definite tempering effect. In the Crimea, summer weather may start in early May and continue until late September. There is little snow in winter. In the Carpathians, the climate is somewhat cooler, but can be qualified as mild anyway, with a winter average of 25°F (-4°C), and warm, pleasant summers of 75°F-80°F (24°C–27°C). The summer heat never lasts for more than a week, and usually, if the temperature goes higher than 85°F, it is considered extremely hot. Long and comfortable springs and autumns are the most enjoyable seasons in Ukraine.

FAUNA

Ukraine's wildlife is typical of steppe and forest areas. Centuries ago there were bears and wolves in the forests, but today the largest predator is the red fox, which can be seen in almost all the woodlands of the country, along with small numbers of wild boar and deer. Smaller animals include badgers, hares, red squirrels, and hedgehogs.

The red fox prefers to live in farmlands and woodlots, making Ukraine a veritable red fox paradise.

Rivers and lakes are the habitat area for muskrat, otter, coypu, and beaver. In the steppes, there are gophers and other small rodents. Ukraine does not have many snakes, however, some venomous vipers can be found in damp or swampy areas. There are several varieties of harmless grass-snakes and lizards.

The steppe eagle is one of the largest Ukrainian birds. Other birds of prey living in different regions of the country include hawks, falcons, and owls. Swallows, bluebirds, and sparrows can be seen in abundance all over the country. In the past, bullfinches were common in the winter, but there are fewer now due to warmer winters and the general pollution of the environment. Wild and domestic pigeons are common in the cities, while in the forests there are magpies and cuckoo-birds. Some lakes, ponds, and reed-covered river banks provide summer homes for a variety of ducks and geese.

Pike, perch, perch-pike, crucian, gudgeon, carp, and many other fresh water fish are common in the rivers, lakes, and ponds in Ukraine. The Black and Azov Seas used to be significant sources for commercial fishing, but over-fishing in the 1950s exhausted the fish supply.

Kreshchatik is Kyiv's main thoroughfare.

ADMINISTRATIVE DIVISIONS

Ukraine is divided into administrative units (the equivalent of states in the United States) called *oblast* ("OB-lahst"). There are 24 oblasts and one autonomous republic—the Crimea. An oblast is a territory with its own borders, government, and capital, called the oblast center, from which the name of the oblast is derived. For example, the capital city of Cherkaska Oblast in central Ukraine is Cherkasy. Each oblast is divided into counties, called *rayon* ("rai-OHN").

CITIES

Ukraine is very densely populated therefore there are a significant number of large cities. In fact, there are six cities with populations over 1,000,000, nearly 20 with populations over 200,000, and more than 50 with populations over 100,000. A Ukrainian would describe a city of less than 100,000 people as small, and an area with less than 5,000 people would not even be called a town.

The capital of Ukraine is Kyiv, with a population of approximately 3,000,000. Kyiv was the center of the first Russian state. As the ancient capital of the Slavs, there are still numerous churches, monasteries, and monuments reflecting Kyiv's golden age. Parliament, the President's headquarters, and the various ministries are all located in Kyiv.

Other large cities with populations over 1,000,000 are Kharkiv, Dnipropetrovsk, and Donetsk in the east, Odesa in the south, and Lviv in the west. Lviv is called the "western capital" of Ukraine because during the Soviet era it was in the west that Ukrainian culture survived. The city was built by the Ukrainian king, Danylo Romanovych, in the 13th century, and named for his son Lev. Due to its location near the border, Lviv has developed a diverse population, architectural styles, and traditions, including Ukrainian, Polish, Jewish, Austrian, and Hungarian.

Kharkiv is the country's main industrial city. The city was originally settled by the Kozaks in the 17th century. Surrounding the city are large deposits of iron ore and coal, which are extracted and then processed in Kharkiv.

A view of the city of Lviv, Ukraine's western capital.

Dnipropetrovsk is another important industrial city located along the bank of the Dnipro River. It is a busy river port and railroad junction.

The main seaport in Ukraine is Odesa, on the northwestern shore of the Black Sea. It is the site of a large shipbuilding industry, and a manufacturing and trading center. There are more than 100 nationalities of people living in this cosmopolitan city.

HISTORY

UKRAINE HAS HAD THE MISFORTUNE of being located at the crossroads of migration, trade, and war for most of its existence. Throughout its 2,000-year history Ukraine's fertile land has attracted numerous invaders. Today, for the first time in its history, Ukraine's territories are united under one government.

THE EARLIEST DAYS

The first signs of people found in the territory of modern Ukraine date back 150,000 years. In the late 19th century, excavations took place in the village of Trypillia, not far from Kyiv. The excavations uncovered evidence of a unique civilization dating from 4500-2000 B.C. It soon became known as the Trypillian civilization. Trypillians lived in communities of about 10,000 people, 15 of them or so sharing two-story log houses, which they built to form a large circle. Hunters and gatherers, the Trypillians smelted bronze and produced mysteriously beautiful objects of art.

In the last millennium B.C., different groups of nomads, Cimmerians, Sarmatians, and Scythians, migrated to the southern part of modern Ukraine. The Scythians especially left evidence of their life in the steppes near the Black Sea coasts. They were very accomplished equestrians and were among the first people to master the art of riding. This mobility gave them a great advantage over their neighbors, allowing them to attack and infiltrate quickly. The Cimmerians, who still fought on foot, soon succumbed to the stronger Scythian

Opposite: **A statue of Lenin still stands in Yalta's town center.**

Below: **The remains of an ancient Scythian capital in Neopol Skifsky.**

15

Three brothers, Kyi, Schek, and Khoriv, are the legendary founders of Kyiv. The city was named after the oldest brother Kyi. Two parts of the city, Schekovytsa and Khorevytsa, were named after Schek and Khoriv. The river was named after their sister Lybid.

cavalry and were forced to flee the plains north of the Black Sea. This series of victories brought great fame to the Scythians, who became very prosperous after settling in the plains. Scythians who established themselves as rulers were given grand burials, and gravesites discovered in the Crimea have uncovered tombs filled with gold and other precious metals. The Scythians were to enjoy this wealth and power until the fourth century B.C., when the Sarmatians appeared on the scene. The Sarmatians continually put pressure on the Scythians until they were confined to the Crimea, gradually supplanting them as the rulers of the steppe, until the second century B.C., when they destroyed the last remnants of this once powerful community.

THE SLAVS

Direct ancestors of modern Ukrainians, called Slavs, moved south into the Black Sea area only in the fifth century A.D. to escape the invading Huns. Slavs originally came from Asia, but migrated to eastern Europe in the third or second millennium B.C. In the fifth and sixth centuries A.D., the westward movement of the Germans stimulated the great migration of the Slavs into present day Ukraine. They originally occupied the area between the Vistula and Dnipro rivers, stretching northward to the Carpathian Mountains. The Slavs began to expand their region, and by the end of the eighth century they had conquered the Balkans as well. The Hungarians occupied the eastern part of the Balkan Peninsula, but they were quickly assimilated to the Slavs and with them were converted to Christianity in the ninth century. An Asian invasion in the ninth century divided the southern Slavs from those of the west and east. The western Slavs (Czechs, Slovaks, Elbe Slavs, Poles, and Pomeranians) received Christianity from the west while the eastern Slavs (White Russians, Russians, and Ukrainians) adhered to the Greek Orthodox Church.

KYIVAN RUS

According to legends in one of the first chronicles, *Tale of Bygone Years*, written by a monk named Nestor in 1113, Kyiv was founded in the seventh century A.D. by Prince Kyi and his family. The community in Kyiv flourished until an attack by the Khazars devastated the territory. In the ninth century, Slavs, who by that time had settled in the region, called on Viking rulers from northern

A portrait of Christian monks painted on the wall of the Lavra monastery in Kyiv.

Europe to assist in the government of Kyiv. The Viking rulers were later killed when Prince Oleg conquered Kyiv in 882 A.D. This was to be the beginning of a line of rulers of the Rurik dynasty. At that time the people of Kyiv were known as the Rus, so the new state established by the Ruriks was called Kyivan Rus.

In the 10th century, Prince Volodymyr, the fourth member of the Rurik dynasty, became the first Christian ruler of Kyivan Rus. Although Christianity had existed in Kyiv long before Volodymyr's time, he had remained a pagan. In 988, Volodymyr embraced Christianity when he married the sister of Byzantine emperor Basil II. In that year he ordered the Christian conversion of Kyiv in a move to unite the Slavic peoples in the region.

Volodymyr's son, Prince Yaroslav, also promoted Christianity as the religion of the Slavs. He built schools and churches, established written laws, and forged ties with neighboring nations by marrying his three sons and three daughters into other royal families. Through his military victories, Yaroslav consolidated the Kyivan state, and made Kyivan Rus into the largest empire in Europe.

It was in 1183 that the word "Ukraine," meaning borderland, first appeared in the chronicles.

STRUGGLE FOR POWER, DEFENCE AGAINST INVADERS

After Yaroslav's death, there was a struggle for power between his three sons. The country was divided into principalities ruled by his offspring, which made it easy prey for invaders, particularly the nomad tribes of the Polovtsy. From 1057 to 1100 Kyivan Rus suffered repeated Polovtsy invasions, which saw Kyiv's decline and the end of the golden period of political stability achieved by Volodymyr and carried on by his son, Yaroslav. During the same period, there was a major shift in trade routes brought on by the First Crusade, making the route between the Baltic and Black Seas superfluous.

In 1223, the Mongols invaded. By that time, the principalities had been at war intermittently for generations, and the Mongols' mounted warriors were too skilful for the Slavs to resist.

After the defeat of the Slavs, the Mongols established a unified political system in an attempt to revive the commerce that had traditionally crossed the Central Asian plains. Although much of the country lay in ruins due to years of fighting, many cities made a surprisingly rapid recovery under the rule of the Mongols. (Kyiv, however, never fully recovered its grandeur.) Administration of the principalities was left in the hands of the Turkic leaders and Muslim merchants who had been operating for generations in the area.

In 1241, the Mongols founded the Golden Horde, a state that extended from the Danube to the Ural River, and at its height included areas such as the Crimea, Bulgaria, Moldova, and parts of Siberia. To avoid further conquest, Ukrainians moved westward and established the state of Galicia-Volhynia. The state remained independent until 1340, when it succumbed to the superior power of Lithuania and Poland.

KOZAKS

Originally runaways from unbearable conditions of life under the landlords, Kozaks formed democratic military communities on the Dnipro River islands. They elected their leaders, lived a life of constant training, and fought against Tatars, Turks, Poles, and Russians. History books and folk songs praise the names of prominent Kozak leaders, called *hetman* ("HET-mahn") in Ukrainian, such as Yevstafiy Dashkevych, Dmytro Vyshnevetskyy, Petro Sagaidachnyy, and Mykhailo Doroshenko. Despite many attempts to disband the Kozaks, the movement continued to exist through to the 18th century.

When Lithuania and Poland united in the 16th century, western Ukraine and the city of Kyiv came under the control of the Polish king. As Polish subjects, Ukrainians were required to learn the Polish language and to accept Roman Catholicism, the Polish faith.

During this time there were numerous uprisings against the Polish and Lithuanian occupiers. Many peasants escaped from their landlords and led dangerous, but free lives. These escapees were called *Kozaks* ("koh-ZAHK," Cossacks in English spelling), a name which is derived from the Turkish word for "a free man."

17TH CENTURY UKRAINE

The strong Kozak army and the system of Hetmanship brought revival to the Ukrainian people and their culture. The Kozak troops had made many successful raids on Moscow (1601, 1616) and in the Crimea (1616, 1628), and fought with the Polish army and the Tatars. The Orthodox Patriarch leadership was restored in 1620, and the first institute for higher learning, called the Kyivan Academy, was founded by Petro Mohyla in 1632.

Besides the regular raids against Poland, several anti-Polish uprisings took place in different parts of Ukraine in 1630, 1635, and 1638. One prominent Kozak leader, Bohdan Khmelnytskyy, initiated an organized anti-Polish movement, which triumphed in several battles, but never completely defeated the Polish army. In 1654, Khmelnytskyy signed the Pereyaslav Treaty, uniting Ukraine with Russia in an effort to oust the Poles from power. The united Kozak-Russian army was a powerful fighting force, however, the Kozaks soon realized that while fighting one oppressor, they appeared to be falling under the thumb of another, even stronger one—Russia.

The monument to Bohdan Khmelnytskyy in Kyiv. Khmelnytskyy signed a very controversial treaty with the Russians that has put him in the history books forever.

In 1708, the leader of the Kozak army, Hetman Ivan Mazepa, left the Russian army and joined Swedish king Karl XII. In the ensuing battle at Poltava, the Swedish-Kozak army was defeated by the Russians, beginning the Russian colonization of Ukraine.

UKRAINE IN THE RUSSIAN EMPIRE

Peter the Great, the tsar of Russia, ruled his Empire with an iron fist. Decrees limiting Ukrainian freedom were issued from the outset. The second part of the century saw the further colonization of Ukraine,with Russia taking over former Polish and Austrian territories.

In the 19th century, the first signs of discontent became visible. A peasant movement for freedom began in 1813, a revolt by nobles (called Decembrists) in Kyiv and Odesa took place in 1825, and prominent Ukrainians raised their voices to restore the rights of the Ukrainian people.

At the same time, the first coal deposits were discovered in eastern Ukraine; the first sugar refineries were built in central Ukraine; the southern cities of Odesa and Mykolayiv were founded; and new universities opened in Kharkiv, Kyiv, and Odesa. Several magazines and newspapers were published in Ukrainian (despite the fact that it was forbidden) and distributed both in Ukraine and abroad. In 1861, under the pressure of the uprisings and the wave of dissatisfaction, serfdom was abolished. Yulian Bachynskyy's article "Ukraina Irredenta," published in 1895, was the first public mention of Ukrainian independence.

Red Guards shooting from an armored car in Petrograd in October 1917, the year of the Russian Revolution.

SOVIET POWER IN UKRAINE

In the early 20th century, poverty and hunger throughout the Russian Empire fuelled a growing national liberation movement in Ukraine, and a growing revolutionary movement in Russia. Revolutionaries, known as Communists, wanted to establish a new kind of government in Russia, and plotted to overthrow the tsar. The leader of the Communists, Vladimir Lenin, promised peace, food, and land to the people. In March 1917, the Communists overthrew the tsar. In November of that year, the Communists seized power in St. Petersburg and Moscow, and the first Ukrainian National Republic was proclaimed in Kyiv by the 3rd Ukrainian Universal Congress. In January, 1918, the Fourth Universal Congress proclaimed Ukraine independent, with sovereign borders, its own currency, a Constitution, and a government. In April, 1918, Mykhailo Hrushevskyy was elected the first President of the Ukrainian National Republic. Lenin's new Communist state, and several other nations, recognized Ukrainian independence.

However, the Republic was short-lived, and with the advance of Soviet Russia's army in 1919, a full-scale civil war erupted and lasted for almost two years. Ukrainian nationals continued their struggle for an independent Ukraine, but by the end of 1920, the "independent" Ukrainian Soviet Socialist Republic had been formed.

FAMINE IN UKRAINE

Ukraine was one of the first areas in the USSR to be targeted for collectivization under Stalin's new agricultural program because it was a grain-surplus-producing region. Wealthy Ukrainian farmers were pronounced *kulaks* ("COO-lacks")—the Soviet label for those who owned a slightly larger than average plot of land with hired labor—and were exiled or executed. Anyone who actively resisted was also labelled kulak and suffered a similar fate. The transition caused terrible disruptions in production, but exorbitant taxes were still demanded from peasants. A drought in 1932-33 caused a famine in which millions died of starvation, but the government refused to admit the existence of the famine and sealed off famine ravaged areas so that relief could not be provided. Nearly 7,000,000 Ukrainians starved to death in less than two years. Everything possible was done to prevent the world from discovering what had really happened in Ukraine. And if they did discover, they were discouraged from believing.

INTEGRATION OF UKRAINE INTO THE SOVIET UNION

According to the treaty between the Russian Soviet Socialist Federation and the Ukrainian Soviet Socialist Republic, signed in December 1920, both countries remained independent, but formed an economic and

Joseph Stalin, former leader of the USSR.

military union. In reality, Ukraine had become Russia's milch cow, providing her with food, coal, and other supplies. Ukrainian culture, economy, and government were gradually brought under the control of Moscow, even more so after the formation of the Union of Soviet Socialist Republics (USSR) in December, 1922.

Intensive industrialization of the eastern areas of Ukraine continued over the next 10 years, and strict measures were taken to reorganize agriculture. The new leader of the USSR, Joseph Stalin, abolished private farms and ordered the creation of state-run collective farms instead. Farmers were forced to give up their land and livestock, and to work as hired labor on government farms. Those who protested were arrested, executed, or sent into exile.

It is estimated that about 8,000,000 Ukrainians were lost as the result of World War II, including 4,000,000 civilians killed and more than 2,000,000 taken to Germany for forced labor.

WORLD WAR II

After the signing of the Molotov-Ribbentrop Pact, which banned any conflict between the USSR and Germany in 1939, both countries made vast territorial gains, including western Ukraine. The new borders were considered sovereign, but both countries were preparing for war. For Ukraine the war started on June 22, 1941 with the German army invading the western borders and bombing Kyiv. Despite the heroic defence of major cities, all of Ukraine was occupied by July, 1942. Some Ukrainians hailed the Germans as their liberators, but it soon became apparent that Ukraine had in no way been liberated. In October, 1942, the Ukrainian Resistance Army was created in Lviv. It fought both the German and the Soviet Armies in the hope of attaining Ukrainian independence. As early as December, 1942, the Soviet Army started its counteroffensive. Ukraine was free from German occupation only in October, 1944.

While restoration of Ukrainian industry and agriculture started immediately after the war, the restoration of its language and culture was still many years off.

MODERN UKRAINE

With new policies of *perestroika* ("pair-a-STROY-ka," restructuring) and *glasnost* ("GLASS-nost," openness) introduced by the first and the last president of the USSR, Mikhail Gorbachev, in 1985, the national renaissance in Ukraine burst out. In April 1986, the Chornobyl nuclear-plant accident added tension to the political situation. In 1987, for the first time in many years, Ukraine celebrated the Millennium anniversary of Christianity. A national democratic movement called *Rukh* ("movement" in Ukrainian) was founded in September, 1989, and the authorities had to register it as a legal political organization in January, 1990 (a significant event in a country with a one-party system). Ukrainian became an official language in October, 1989. Events of a similar nature were happening all over the Soviet Union.

Former Soviet president, Mikhail Gorbachev.

In August, 1991, an attempt by reactionary Communists to overthrow Gorbachev urged the majority of the republics that comprised the Soviet Union to ban the Communist Party. On August 24, 1991, Ukrainian Parliament declared Ukraine independent. A national vote took place on December 1, 1991, and an overwhelming majority (about 90%) of Ukrainians voted for independence.

The same month Mikhail Gorbachev resigned and the USSR ceased to exist. Leonid Kravchuk, a former high-ranking Communist, became the first president of Ukraine. He prompted several important reforms, but lost his position to Leonid Kuchma, who was elected the second president of Ukraine in July, 1994.

GOVERNMENT

SINCE THE FALL OF THE SOVIET UNION, Ukraine has become an independent republic for the second time in its long history. Today, Ukrainians participate actively in the government of their country, taking advantage of the freedom to become involved in the decisions affecting their land, their children, and their homes. Ukraine is now an active supporter of nuclear disarmament, and has refused to house nuclear weapons in its territory. The government attempts to solve problems of all kinds peacefully and democratically.

LEGISLATION

The legislative body of the country is the Supreme Council, or *Verkhovna Rada* ("ver-KHOV-nah RAH-dah"). The Verkhovna Rada is a unicameral parliament that adopts its decisions based on the votes of its members from various political parties. The members of the Verkhovna Rada are called deputies, and are elected by the people for a term of four years. A deputy can be recalled from his or her duties by the electorate if he or she is judged not to be fulfilling due obligations.

Both Mariinsky Palace, the president's headquarters (above), and the Verkhovna Rada (opposite) are located in Kyiv. In fact, both buildings are located in the same complex.

A new constitution has been the theme of debates in the Supreme Council for several years. The temporary provisions of the present constitution are no longer satisfactory in the minds of most Ukrainians. Issues such as private ownership (of particular importance in Ukraine, where most people make their livelihood from the land) need to be reviewed if there is to be a new constitution. New laws based on the existing constitution, as well as any amendments to it, are adopted by the Verkhovna Rada.

FEDERAL GOVERNMENT

Carrying out the laws and decrees of the Verkhovna Rada is the duty of the federal government, represented by the Council of Ministers and the various ministries. The prime minister is the head of the Council of Ministers, appointed to his position upon the recommendation of a

specially organized committee in the Verkhovna Rada, and with the confirmation of its deputies. Independence has seen the emergence of new ministries to deal with pressing issues, such as the Ministry of Environmental Protection. Another new addition is the Service for National Security, which has replaced the Ukrainian branch of the Soviet Union's Committee for State Security, better known as the KGB.

Leonid Kravchuk became Ukraine's first president in 1991.

EXECUTIVE POWER

The president of Ukraine, the chief executive of the country, is elected by universal, equal, and direct suffrage by secret ballot for a term of five years. The president retains the right to veto decisions made by the deputies of the Supreme Council. The president cannot be elected for more than two successive terms.

The first president of Ukraine, Leonid Kravchuk, was elected almost unanimously, since he was the Chairman of the Verkhovna Rada and initiated Ukraine's independence decree in August, 1991. He also supported the banning of the Communist Party, despite the fact that in Soviet Ukraine he possessed one of the top positions in the Ukrainian Communist Party.

The first completely democratic, all-Ukrainian presidential elections were held in 1994, when President Kravchuk lost to the current president, Leonid Kuchma. Mr. Kuchma was mainly supported in eastern and southern Ukraine, while in the west he was reproached as a man with "pro-Russian" attitudes. President Kuchma has instituted several strong reforms in his term to date.

The current president of Ukraine, Leonid Kuchma.

Special militia forces are often on site for the appearance of important people, like the president.

"Even when good laws were adopted, there was an enormous gap between what the law said and how it was enforced."

–Larisa Afanasyeva, a Russian legal scholar (New York Times, December 9, 1989).

LAW AND ORDER

Direct enforcement of laws is handled by the *militsya* ("mih-LIH-tsiah"), the Ukrainian police, under the auspices of the Ministry of Home Affairs. Militiamen wearing dark blue uniforms and armed with handguns and clubs can be seen walking through the streets of Ukrainian cities, or cruising in highway patrol cars. Recently, special militia forces armed with automatic weapons have also appeared.

Decades of confrontation between the people and the government has created a very suspicious attitude towards law enforcement bodies. Ukrainians do not trust the authorities in general. The totalitarian past has reinforced these attitudes and in general people adhere to the philosophy that involving the police brings more trouble than good. As a result, people try to resolve conflicts among themselves, calling for the police only when there is no other option.

THE MILITARY

A mandatory two year military service is required for all men in good health, starting from the age of 18. There are some exemptions from military service: those who are the only child to support elderly parents, those with serious health problems, or those with a family of their own and at least two children born before drafting age. College students are sometimes exempted, depending on the political trends in the Verkhovna Rada. Professional military men and women join the armed forces after graduating from military academies, or without special education if they apply voluntarily. Military service is voluntary for women.

Gun ownership laws in Ukraine are very strict, and only militiamen and women and the armed forces are permitted to carry guns.

LOCAL GOVERNMENT

The structure of local government is hierarchical, with the federal government at the top of the ladder. Below that are oblasts with their own government (the oblast administration) as well as a local version of Parliament called the Oblast Council of People's Deputies. Elections to the Oblast Council are held every four years, with balloting deputies representing a division within their oblast. The oblast administration is responsible for local government affairs, but since its powers are limited, it very often only enforces the decisions of the federal government. The head of the oblast administration is the Chairman of the Oblast Executive Committee, a position which changes quite often.

Rayon (county) government is a smaller model of the oblast government, but carries even less autonomy.

The first free election in Ukraine gave Ukrainians a new sense of power in their ability to change the status quo.

A city council represents the interests of people living in cities and towns. The chairperson of the city council, comparable to a mayor, is elected by the population of the city at large. It is the chairperson's duty to select an executive committee, members of which are approved or rejected by the city council.

The feature characteristic of local governments and their auxiliary offices is parallel subordination. An office such as the Department of Agriculture of an oblast (or rayon) is subordinate to the Oblast Council of People's Deputies on one hand, and the Ministry of Agriculture on the other, leaving it with very little room for decision-making. Local authorities

face a constant struggle to free themselves from the influence of higher powered offices. One of the most urgent problems is determining how tax money should be divided between the offices.

After years of living under a one-party system in the Soviet Union, it is not surprising that Ukrainians do not believe that they can effectively influence political events. Fortunately, attitudes like these are gradually changing. Since independence dozens of new parties reflecting new views and political beliefs have arisen to fill the void of the Communist Party. One of the most important and influential parties, *Rukh* ("rookh"), was founded as early as 1989. Rukh (literally, "movement") is a Ukrainian nationalist party. In 1990, Rukh organized a human chain across a 300-mile (484-km) stretch of highway to protest the Soviet occupation of Ukraine. Five hundred thousand Ukrainians joined the chain to express their discontent.

With the first free election taking place in 1993, Ukrainians are beginning to be more optimistic about the power to promote new ideas through politics.

In this new era, people are free to criticize the government although many are wary of doing so.

ECONOMY

UKRAINE IS ONE OF the richest nations in the world in terms of natural resources. Before independence, Ukraine produced 25% of the USSR's industrial output, 25% of its agricultural output, 30% of its meat, and 50% of its iron ore. And yet, today, Ukraine is in a state of deep economic crisis.

An overwhelming majority of Ukraine's people voted for independence not only because they wanted the freedom of cultural expression, but also because they wanted to be masters of their land and resources. Expectations of immediate prosperity, however, were soon dampened and Ukrainians have been forced to come to terms with the sobering reality of the economic situation. The economy was badly mismanaged by the Soviet state. Despite years of abuse, the rich black soil that has made Ukraine famous as the "breadbasket" of Europe still yields rich harvests, however, lack of technology prevents the crops from being processed effectively. In

some cases the crops never reach the processing units because the transportation system is inadequate, particularly when the weather is rainy. Because of these problems, Ukraine lost about 30% of its record harvest in 1993.

Natural gas and oil deposits have been almost exhausted because of intensive use by Soviet industry. Worse than this is people's attitude. Years of living under a regime that discouraged initiative taught people to believe that attempts to improve the status quo are nothing short of harmful. One of the first reforms that Ukrainian leaders undertook was to privatize a number of enterprises.

A state-run steel plant in Kryvyy Rig.

STATE VERSUS PRIVATE

The best way to praise a Ukrainian is to call them a good *khazyayin* ("kha-ZIA-yin") for a man or *khazyayka* ("kha-ZIAI-ka") for a woman—a good master of the household. This is a reflection of the Ukrainian desire to manage their property as well as possible. The state-run economy discouraged such desires, which is why early Ukrainian reforms included privatization. Privatization and newly created private enterprises have caused a dramatic increase in the number of industrial enterprises in Ukraine—from 6,850 in 1992 to 8,826 in 1994. In most cases, new businesses were relatively small, but covered a wide range of industries including 2,507 food industry enterprises, 1,984 machine building and metal processing enterprises, and 1,003 construction enterprises. A significantly smaller number of enterprises (208) are involved in chemical industry, but almost all of them, like the factories in Cherkasy or Rivne, are gigantic facilities with between 3,000 and 5,000 employees. Privatization of most state-controlled enterprises has taken more time than was initially expected. In 1994, only 2,678 enterprises out of 8,826 had been privatized.

FAR ABROAD AND NEAR ABROAD

A loose unity of former Soviet states called the Commonwealth of Independent States (CIS) was created in 1992 after the dissolution of the USSR. In that year, Ukraine imported US$39 billion worth of products from "near abroad," the term used to describe the countries of the CIS, in comparison with only US$5.1 billion from "far abroad," or the rest of the world. It exported only US$36 billion worth of goods near abroad and US$3.6 billion far abroad. Ukrainian grain was the main product for export, together with sugar, sunflowers, and meat. Heavy industry products, such as steel and textiles, are auxiliary export products in comparison with agricultural ones. Ukraine imports oil, gas, and paper from Russia and Turkmenistan, otherwise it is self-sufficient.

An import-export shipyard at Yalta.

UNEMPLOYMENT

Unable to find jobs in the conventional workforce, many Ukrainians have turned to self-employment. This man is a money changer.

In the Soviet Union, employment was not only a right, it was also a duty. According to Soviet law, at least one member of the family had to work. Anyone who violated this law faced punishment, sometimes resulting in imprisonment.

With the recent attempts at transformation to a free-market economy, the level of unemployment has increased dramatically. This is explained by changes in the infrastructure of the industrial and agricultural complex, but it is also very likely due to the greater degree of emphasis being put on efficiency—there is no longer any reason to hire two people to do the job of one.

In 1995, the rate of unemployment was 0.29%, or 82,200 people. This does not seem high compared to other nations, but this figure only refers to the number of people who addressed the unemployment bureaus. These bureaus are relatively new institutions for Ukrainians, who are accustomed to relying on themselves for employment, therefore it is estimated that the actual number of unemployed is three times this amount.

There is a dangerous trend toward women's unemployment: 59,800 out of the 82,200 who registered at the unemployment bureaus were women.

TRANSPORTATION

The railway system in Ukraine has been developed to the highest level. There is hardly a town in Ukraine with a population over 10,000 that does not have a railway station, both for cargo and passenger trains. Every day, thousands of 80–100-car trains carry goods and raw materials to various destinations in Ukraine.

Waterways are also used intensively for transportation needs. Major rivers, such as the Dnipro, the Dnister, the Privdennyy Bug, and the Azov and Black seas serve as transport routes for ships and barges year round. The Black Sea Shipping Company (BLASCO) is one of the largest transportation enterprises in the world.

Airways are not used as widely as they were in the past. Lack of fuel, insufficient planes (most Soviet planes remained the property of the Soviet air transport company, *Aeroflot,* in Russia), and high cost are just two of the reasons. In large cities there are buses, trams, streetcars, and subways. Public transportation is inexpensive and efficient, but during rush hour, passengers can be packed as tightly as sardines.

UKRAINIAN CURRENCY

In January, 1992, a temporary "transition period" currency was introduced to replace the Russian ruble, the currency used across the former Soviet Union. The Ukrainian word for the temporary currency is *karbovanets* ("kahr-BOH-vah-nets"), though it is often called "coupon." When the coupons were first introduced there were only 1, 3, 5, 10, 25, 50, and 100 karbovanet notes. Later on, because of hyperinflation, these notes became a collector's item. By the first quarter of 1996, the smallest bill was 1,000, and the largest 10,000,000.

The rate of exchange in 1996 was approximately 150,000 karbovanets to the US dollar, so even 10 million karbovanets equalled only US$68.

In the third quarter of 1996, the Ukrainian government was finally able to introduce the new Ukrainian currency, called the *hryvna* ("HRIV-nah"). It remains to be seen whether or not the economy will be able to support the new currency, but Ukrainians are optimistic.

MANUFACTURING

"Made in Ukraine" labels are not commonly seen on products that can be bought on the shelves in the United States. Ukrainian-made goods that are exported to foreign markets are jackets, women's apparel, and mineral fertilizers, but many other Ukrainian products have not found a world consumer yet. A variety of goods, however, are manufactured for the internal market. One of the largest tractor factories is located in Kharkiv. Trucks are produced in Kryvyy Rig. Small cars are made in Zaporizhzhya, buses in Lviv, television sets in Symferopil, Kyiv, Smila, and Lviv. In total, about 33,400 trucks, 8,500 buses, and 134,500 cars are manufactured annually. Ukraine has a strong base for machine building in a variety of industries.

Every year 2,909,000 metric tons of mineral fertilizers are produced for internal and foreign markets, as well as a significant amount of synthetic fabric, yarn, and polymeric plastic.

In the 1930s, academician Yevhen Paton introduced the unique technology of whole-welded bridge construction. Several bridges of this kind can be seen on the Dnipro River; many more were built throughout the Soviet Union.

AGRICULTURE

Agriculture accounts for 32% of Ukraine's net economic output and involves approximately 20% of the nation's labor force. Ukraine has 75 million acres (29 million hectares) of arable soil. While this figure at one time accounted for only 15% of all arable land in the former Soviet Union, Ukraine once produced nearly 25% of the USSR's grain, 55% of its beets, 45% of its oilseed, and 22% of its meat.

The three main components for agricultural success in Ukraine according to Ukrainians are the hard-working farmers, the moderate climate, and the most fertile black soil in the world—*chornozem* ("chor-noh-ZEM"). Thanks to these three gifts, Ukraine produces 50 million metric tons of grain, 44 million tons of sugar beets, 18 million tons of potatoes, 7.5 million tons of vegetables, and 2.7 million tons of sunflowers annually. Livestock production, mainly hogs, beef, and poultry, accounts for 54% of the value of gross agricultural output.

The struggle to privatize farms in Ukraine continues. In 1993, private household plots produced 35% of all agricultural products, collective farms, 40%, and state farms, 25%.

Despite the natural richness of the soil, the country is still not meeting its potential. There is usually a shortage of materials, such as fertilizer, pesticides, animal feed, machinery, and spare parts for existing machinery that prevent maximum output. As a result, Ukrainian crop yields are, on average, only 50%-55% of those in the West.

COLLECTIVE, STATE, AND PRIVATE FARMING

Under the rules of the Soviet state-run economy, private farming was banned. The only private farming allowed was conducted on small 2-acre (4 square m) plots that qualified more as gardens than fields. Collective farms were the norm under the administration of the USSR, with combined ownership of the land, and, in theory, combined ownership of everything produced on the land. Today, a growing movement to reintroduce private farming is forcing the government to issue laws that will ensure private land ownership. Ukrainians are attempting to create the basis for the re-emergence of family farming.

Until 1992, state and collective farms accounted for 92% of the best agricultural lands, but produced only 69% of the gross agricultural product. Today, private household plots, both in rural and urban areas, represent only 6% of the arable land, yet account for 30% of livestock production and 20% of crop production. Despite these figures the government is reluctant to support reforms favoring private farming.

THE CHORNOBYL DISASTER

On April 26, 1986, one of the reactors at the Chornobyl nuclear power plant exploded, causing the radioactive contamination of huge territories surrounding the area. About nine tons of nuclear reactive materials were discharged into the air, polluting major parts of Kyiv (which is 60 miles, 97 km to the south), Rivne, and Chernihiv. All together, about 25,000 square miles (64,750 square km) of land inhabited by 2.5 million people were affected. Many of the inhabitants have already been evacuated, but it is estimated that about 700,000 people still need to be evacuated from polluted areas. Long term effects on the genetic health of the nation are not completely clear yet, but many people died as a result of contamination during the days of direct exposure.

The desperate need for energy caused Ukrainian Parliament to vote to keep the rest of the Chornobyl reactors running until 2010, when their life-span is over.

ENERGY

In Soviet Ukraine, there was no need to think about energy—the cost per kilowatt of electricity was a fraction of a cent and gasoline cost 30 cents per gallon (8 cents per liter). In those days, there were significant deposits of natural gas and oil in the Carpathian Mountains, but over the years these were almost completely exhausted to supply the rest of the Soviet Union with energy. Ukraine soon became dependent on other sources of energy—hydroelectric power, coal burning, and nuclear power. A number of dams have been built on major rivers (the first one, called Dniproges, in 1932). In most cases, however, the end result has been the re-formation of the rivers, leading to devastating floods and massive evacuations.

Coal burning facilities do not produce great amounts of power and therefore serve limited areas. They are also very harmful to the environment since the by-product is the primary source of acid rain.

Today, Ukraine is in a critical condition in terms of energy. Lack of oil and natural gas has increased the dependence on nuclear power. In 1985, only 19.6% of all electricity in Ukraine was produced by nuclear power stations. By 1994, Ukrainian nuclear power stations were producing 34.3% of all electricity in the country. Yet despite these increases, electricity has to be shut down every day for several hours in many regions of Ukraine in order to decrease consumption.

UKRAINIANS

DESPITE INVASION AND OCCUPATION by foreign conquerors and the number of minorities living in the country, Ukrainians have maintained their predominantly Slavic features. This is not so surprising considering there has been no significant immigration to Ukraine throughout its history. On the contrary, quite a remarkable number of Ukrainians can be found throughout the world. Emigrants have had several reasons for leaving home—escaping political oppression, cruel landlords, and unbearable economic circumstances. Massive emigration from Ukraine occurred at the beginning of this century, when continuous turmoil in Russia caused many people to search for better living conditions abroad.

Opposite: **A Ukrainian woman with typical Slavic features.**

Below: **This girl is one of the large group of Russians living in Ukraine.**

After the Communists took over in Ukraine, there were a number dissidents who preferred (or were forced) to live abroad rather than submit to Communist rule. The largest number of Ukrainians abroad live in Canada, followed by the United States.

Despite the large numbers of people who have emigrated from Ukraine, it is still one of the most densely populated countries in Europe. In 1995, the population of the country was 52.7 million, 68% of whom lived in urban areas. The majority of the population identify themselves as Ukrainians (73%). The second largest group is Russian (22%). Minorities represented by 100,000 people or more are Moldovans, Poles, Jews, Belarussians, Bulgarians, Hungarians, and Romanians.

A Hutsul man with his cow in the Carpathian Mountains.

MINORITIES

Ethnically-speaking, Ukraine is a fairly homogeneous society. However, there are a number of small groups living in the central and southwestern area who differ from mainstream Ukrainians, although they are related ethnically. The Lemky are the most western of these ethnic groups. Until 1946, the Lemky lived throughout the Carpathian Mountains on both the eastern and western sides. Now they are confined to a small area in the westernmost part of Ukraine. It was only recently that the Lemky exchanged their traditional dress, called *chuhy* ("CHOO-hee," a woollen covering without sleeves), for modern clothes.

The Boiky are mountaineers who live slightly further east than the Lemky. Their main occupation is cattle breeding. The Boiky have maintained many of their ancient customs, particularly architecture. The area which they inhabit is spotted with old style churches and wooden houses with large entrance halls. Even today it is not uncommon to see a Boiky man or woman dressed in a traditional long cloak decorated with beads, and tilling the soil using traditional agricultural tools.

The Volhynians inhabit the northern mountain areas. They are known for their musical talents, particularly lyre-playing and singing. Their festive carols and religious songs have been particularly well preserved.

The most notable of the ethnic minorities are the Hutsuls, who breed cattle and sheep and are heavily involved in forestry. They are known throughout Ukraine for their exceptional craftsmanship and building techniques. Wood carving, pottery, brasswork, and rug-weaving are also highly developed Hutsul crafts. For hundreds of years, the Hutsuls have carved objects made of wood, such as doors, chests, and crosses, with intricate geometric patterns and beaded inlay. Today these handicrafts are sold throughout Ukraine, some going for very high prices.

A makeshift cabin atop the Carpathian Mountains used by a Hutsul family when they bring their cattle to pasture.

THE TATARS

The Turkic peoples can be divided into two main groups, the eastern Turks and the western Turks. The eastern Turks, which include people living in Turkey and the regions of the former Soviet Union, including Crimea, can be described as dark-skinned, but many are as fair as western Europeans. Tatars consist of two groups, those living in the former Tatar Autonomous Soviet Socialist Republic (ASSR), located in the middle of the Volga River basin, and those inhabiting the Crimean Peninsula. The Crimean Peninsula was formed into the Crimean ASSR in 1921, and was populated primarily by Tatars. In 1944 the republic was abolished, and the Tatars were deported to Siberia and Central Asia for allegedly collaborating with the Nazis.

Although officially rehabilitated in 1967, the Crimean Tatars were not permitted to return, and it is only now, after the break up of the Soviet Union, that they are beginning to return to their homeland.

The Tatars are well-known as traders, but they also have an ancient tradition of craftsmanship in wood, ceramics, leather, cloth, and metal. During the 9th–15th centuries, the Tatar economy became based on a combination of farming and herding, which continues to this day. As a medieval power, the Tatars had a complex social organization with distinct classes. At the head of the government stood the khan.

This young Tatar boy is copying from the Koran. The Tatars were converted to Islam in the 14th century, and as Sunnites, were instrumental in bringing Islam to Turkistan. Many Tatars, however, have maintained pre-Islamic beliefs in spirits which inhabit the forests, the water, and the household.

NATIONAL FEATURES

The well-known expression *schyryy ukrayinets* ("SHCHIH-riy ook-rah-YI-nets"), meaning sheer Ukrainian, is more a reflection of the dominant features of the Ukrainian character than of physical features.

A typical Ukrainian may have dark or blond hair, and gray, blue or brown eyes, and as a people their personalities may be just as different. But one thing that all Ukrainians are taught from the time they are young is to be hospitable.

When there is a guest in the house, whether it be for several hours or several days, the host's personal life is sacrificed almost completely. In these cases, many Ukrainians will take leave from their jobs, and provide the guest with the best possible accommodation, even if it means temporarily giving up their bedroom.

Feeding a guest is also part of being hospitable, and no expense is spared to be sure the meal is well-prepared and the guest well-fed. Children are taught at a young age that providing a good meal for a guest, whether they are expected or unexpected, is the most important obligation as far as hospitality is concerned.

Many visitors have left Ukraine with the mistaken impression that Ukrainians eat like kings and queens every night of the week.

The hard-working nature of the people is another national feature. It is not uncommon to see men and women over 70 years old still working in Ukraine.

Typical Ukrainian festival dress is colorful and intricately designed.

NATIONAL DRESS

National dress for both women and men is characterized by intricate embroidery and distinct variations in style, depending on the district of Ukraine. Today Ukrainian national dress is worn only for folk festivals.

Men's dress is simpler than that of women. It consists of very loose trousers, held tight at the waist by a sash and at the ankles by laces, and a flaxen shirt with long sleeves. Depending on the season, men may wear an overcoat with long wide sleeves, and a hat that looks something like a stocking cap. The boots are made of whole-leather and worn to the knee. All the garments are worn loose to provide for ease in movement, rather than to underline the features of the figure. This is because Ukrainian national dress dates back to the time of the Kozaks when clothes had to be loose and convenient for fighting.

Traditionally, women wore long skirts, shirts, vests, and coats. It was easy to tell a married woman from an unmarried one since orthodox rules obliged a married woman to cover her hair with a kerchief. Unmarried girls, on the other hand, wore colorful ribbons in their hair as decoration. Coral beads were worn around the neck as part of the outfit, and since a string of such beads was sometimes equal to the price of a cow, the number of strands a woman wore was an indicator of the wealth of her family.

When performing traditional Ukrainian dances, women wear a unique style of dress. A brightly colored woollen skirt is worn over a petticoat, and covered with a white apron. A white embroidered blouse with a vest is worn on top. On their head, the women wear a floral headdress with streamers flowing down the back.

In western Ukraine, there are some significant differences in national dress. This can be explained by the influence of neighboring Hungary, Poland, and Romania. Thus, men wore tight pants, sometimes vests, and tight overcoats. Their hats were round, with moderately wide rims, and decorated with rooster's feathers.

Today women dress comfortably to work in the fields during the hot summer days. The traditional kerchief is still worn on the head for married women.

SENSE OF HUMOR

According to some people, hard times are instrumental in helping people to develop a sense of humor. In the old days, when things got rough, people laughed at themselves and each other as a shield against misfortune, for laughing was one thing that was affordable for everyone.

If this is the case, it is easy to understand why Ukrainians have a very keen sense of humor. Ukrainian humor deals with a variety of situations, from laughing at oneself to satirizing the government (once considered very risky business). The ability to tell jokes well is highly appreciated by Ukrainians.

The city of Odesa has always been the center of humor, not only for Ukraine, but for the USSR as a whole. Regardless of government restrictions, humor festivals were held annually on the 1st of April in Odesa. Since independence these festivals have become huge events that attract thousands of visitors to Odesa each year.

UKRAINIAN NAMES

Ukrainian names are partially of Slavic origin, partially of Biblical origin, sometimes borrowed from Greece (because of the Byzantine influence) and, recently, adopted from other European nations.

Names of Slavic origin date to pagan times, and usually reflect the qualities for which men and women were praised in those times. For example, Svitlana, meaning full of light, and Liudmyla, meaning loved by people, Volodymyr, meaning world owner, and Myroslav, meaning praised by the community, are all popular Slavic names.

Sometimes Ukrainian pronunciation disguises the relation of Ukrainian names to English names, for example, John in English is Ivan in Ukrainian, and Mary is Mariya.

Ukrainian last names are derived from male ancestors' names. Of course, it is difficult to find a family who can trace its family name all the way back to the originator, but it is possible to presume that Ivanchuk definitely had a male ancestor named Ivan. Other names, such as, Kovalchuk, a direct equivalent of the name Smith, were derived from professional skills.

Ukrainians do not have middle names. Instead, they use patronymic names, which are formed by adding a suffix to the name of the person's father. For example, the patronymic name of a woman whose father's name is Ivan, is Ivanivna; a man's patronymic name in this case is Ivanovych. When meeting someone for the first time in Ukraine it is polite to call them by their first and patronymic names rather than using only the first name or last name.

HOW UKRAINIANS ARE CHARACTERIZED

Throughout the Soviet Union, Ukrainians were often thought of as provincial, particularly by Russians. Some Russians still refer to Ukrainian men as home-bound farmers, who save as much as can be saved and are too cautious to have fun. Correspondingly, Ukrainian women are sometimes thought of as simple housewives who are not interested in events outside the home, a stereotype of mythical proportions considering the majority of women in Ukraine work outside the home.

People living in eastern Ukraine are believed to be involved almost exclusively in the mining industry, and to drink more alcohol than other Ukrainians. The population of the city of Odesa is considered to be very entrepreneurial and lazy, but with a superior sense of humor. People in western Ukraine are famous for their conservatism, hard-working character, and ultranationalism.

"What is an optimist?" a Ukrainian once asked. "A person who sees only the bright side of life." "Then what is a pessimist?" "A well-informed optimist."
Life under the Soviet regime taught Ukrainians to be very cautious about new action by the government, even if it seemed beneficial.

Svetlana Savitskaya is a modern Ukrainian who has made a name for herself internationally as a cosmonaut.

FAMOUS UKRAINIANS

Ukraine's history as a satellite state under Russia and the Soviet Union made it difficult for prominent Ukrainians to be recognized. Those who did become famous were almost always directly connected with Ukraine's struggle for independence. Lesya Ukrayinka (1871-1913) took her last name from her beloved country. Many of this poet's works were dedicated to the movement for liberation, as well as expressions of love for her mother and for the Motherland itself.

Two prominent leaders in the 17th century, Hetman Bohdan Khmelnytskyy (1595-1657) and Hetman Ivan Mazepa (1639-1709) were both involved in attempts to liberate Ukraine. Khmelnytskyy entered into a union with Russia to eliminate continuing threats from Poland. Mazepa tried to liberate Ukraine from Russia by forming an alliance with Charles XII of Sweden. These two names can be found in every Ukrainian history book.

In the city of Smila (which means brave) there is a legend of a brave young girl who sacrificed her life to warn Ukrainian defenders of the approaching Mongol troops. In Kam'yanets-Podilskyy, a tragic and beautiful legend describes the story of 400 girls who tied their braids together and leapt down from the walls of the fortress to avoid being enslaved.

TARAS HRYHOROVYCH SHEVCHENKO (1814-1861)

In nearly every household in Ukraine there are two books: the Bible and *Kobzar* (The Bard) by Taras Shevchenko. Shevchenko was born into a family of peasants in central Ukraine. From his early childhood he showed signs of genius. His love for his people and his enormous talent (he was a poet, a painter, and an engraver) turned a son of illiterate serfs into the educated prophet of the Ukrainian people, a creator of Ukrainian literary language, and an inspiration for all generations of fighters for Ukrainian independence. Monuments to Shevchenko have been erected in nearly every town, and anywhere in the world where there is a significant population of Ukrainians. There is a beautiful monument in Washington D.C., erected by Ukrainian Americans acknowledging the poet's achievements.

"And in the great new family, / The family of the free, / With softly spoken, kindly word / Remember also me."

—From Shevchenko's Testament *addressed to the world in the hope that one day the world's family would be free.*

LIFESTYLE

UKRAINE HAS AN AGRICULTURAL HERITAGE, but the majority of its population is urban. Recent migration to urban centers has caused tremendous population growth in the cities. The reason for urban migration is usually standard of living. In the city one can enjoy concert theaters, movie theaters, shopping centers, restaurants, a developed system of public transportation, central heating, direct long distance telephone dialing, and cable television. In the country, there are no concert halls, few movie theaters, no public transportation, no cable television (and television in general is limited to one or two channels), no central heating (which means in many cases utilizing coal and wood stoves), and no telephones, or, for the few people who have them, limited options for placing long distance calls.

Opposite: **Bringing home a wagon of apples from an orchard in the Carpathian Mountains.**

Below: **A village house in western Ukraine.**

In the country, the roads are dry and dusty in the summer, muddy in the autumn and spring, and deep in snow and ice in the winter. Shopping is limited to one or two small convenience stores. Since few people own their own car, trips to a city are rare and tiresome. Recent fuel shortages have made bus schedules unreliable and transportation service costly.

The cities provide a wide range of education options. There are no colleges whatsoever in rural areas, which means in order to pursue a career other than farming or mining, Ukrainians must travel to the city to study. Taking everything into consideration, many people sacrifice the advantages of rural life—fresh air, natural food, low crime rates, and a quiet pace of life—for a more hectic, but more convenient lifestyle in the cities.

A street of old apartment blocks in Lviv.

A HOUSE OR AN APARTMENT?

In rural areas, Ukrainians live in private houses. Although this may seem like a luxury to some, Ukrainians who live in houses do not do so necessarily by choice. There are no apartment blocks outside the large cities in Ukraine. With the recent growth in urban areas, adequate housing has become a problem. Because the socialist order claimed to provide free services to its citizens, theoretically, housing was free for everyone. Registering with the city administration was all any citizen needed to do to be assigned a place to live.

Of course, the standards were very low and many families shared one bedroom, but some apartments had the advantage of some modern conveniences, such as indoor bathrooms and central heating. Though apartments like these were owned by the city, the rent was insignificant and the utilities were very cheap. The catch was to acquire the apartment as soon as possible, because in some cases the waiting list consisted of a thousand names. In these cases a family had to live with parents, or rent an apartment from private owners, which could cost up to 25% of a family's monthly income, for ten years or more.

Private ownership was discouraged since construction and repair materials were either in short supply or unbearably expensive, and services were difficult to obtain. Even if building a house were an option, people preferred to live in an apartment where they were only responsible for maintaining the interior.

After independence, occupants had the option to buy or sell apartments they had been living in. Many families could not afford the upkeep of larger apartments because utilities have become very expensive, so they had to sell their apartments and buy smaller ones. For some, the living conditions were worse, but for others just the knowledge of owning their own home was enough.

DERYBASIVSKA STREET

Derybasivska Street is the main thoroughfare in downtown Odesa, the port-city on the Black Sea. The street has had an unusual fate. After the Revolution of 1917, street names were changed to honor Soviet functionaries. In 1920, Derybasivska Street, named to commemorate one of Odesa's honorary citizens, General DeRibas, was renamed Lassalya Street, in honor of one of the revolutionaries. Plates with the new name replaced old ones on the walls of the houses along the street. But by morning the plates had disappeared, and chalk and paint had been used to inscribe the old name. Numerous attempts to rename the street failed, and finally the Soviet authorities gave up. Thus, Derybasivska Street has kept its name throughout the decades, much to the pride of the city's population.

Soviet state policy transformed the suburbs of large cities into giant apartment housing complexes. Today, apartment buildings consisting of between five and 16 stories stretch for miles. Ukrainians call the buildings "ant colonies." More and more people prefer the idea of owning detached houses. Unfortunately, for the overwhelming majority, a decent house in the city is still beyond affordable.

BACKYARD FARMING

Wages earned from working on a collective farm very rarely satisfy the needs of the average Ukrainian family, and while members of a collective farm enjoy discount prices for products produced on-site, there is rarely enough to spare for anything but food. The solution for many families is to plant a small plot of land near the house, a kind of an extended backyard with an orchard, a cow or two in the barn, several chickens, and three or four pigs. This type of private farming helps collective farmers support their families because the surplus can be sold at the farmers' market in the nearest county seat town.

Even those living in small towns in private houses have begun to use their backyards for farming, if not for additional income, then for fresh vegetables, eggs, and meat for their tables.

Making a hay stack in the backyard.

UKRAINIAN WOMEN

Gender based discrimination is against the law, but Ukraine still has a long way to go before the sexes are truly equal. A woman in Ukraine would be very fortunate indeed if her husband helped her in the kitchen to say nothing of taking complete care of cleaning the house and running other errands, like shopping for food—an exhausting, daily obligation. Instead, the principle that "he brings home the money, she runs the home"

is widely practiced. The irony of this is that Ukraine's economy makes it impossible for a man to earn enough to support his entire family, which means that wives must carry a double load.

In business, women in executive positions are rare, and the percentage of women in Parliament is insignificant. The situation is slightly better at the oblast and city levels of administration. Traditional "homemaking occupations" are still the most common professions for women: preschool teachers, pediatricians, and cooks.

Although Ukraine is still in many senses a traditional society in its treatment of women, in recent years, there have been several laws passed by the Ukrainian government to broaden women's rights. A recent decree by the Ukrainian Parliament allows women to take maternity leave from their jobs for up to three years. During these three years a mother receives a small sum of money from the state each month, called "milk money," in place of her salary. After three years have passed, an employer cannot refuse her the job upon her return.

Also under the law, a father can receive sick leave from work to stay home with an ill child, although in practice it very rarely happens since the mother is usually responsible for such duties.

LIFE CYCLE

In the last 30 years, the average family size in Ukraine has declined from five members to three. This decline is because many couples postpone having children until they own a place of their own. Since housing costs are exorbitant, most young couples continue to live with their parents.

Despite these restrictions, the birth of a child is a most joyous occasion. If finances allow, Ukrainians prefer the new mother to stay at home for as long as possible. However, in many cases, a mother must return to work, particularly if the long break jeopardizes her career. In these cases the family must look elsewhere for child-care. Since it is still common for three generations to live under the same roof, the responsibility of looking after the children falls on the grandparents. In cases where grandparents do not live with their children, parents can turn to a well-developed network of child-care centers.

In Ukraine, babies can be admitted to child-care centers when they are only 11 months old, but most parents, unless it is absolutely necessary, prefer to start using day-care centers only once the child has reached two or three years.

Unlike in many other countries, Ukrainian children are legally obliged to support their elderly or disabled parents. Of course, it is a moral obligation that children are taught when they are young, so legal action is rare. Retirement facilities in Ukraine are exclusively state-run, and for the most part conditions in such facilities are poor.

In some cities, community centers are run by the church to give older children a place to go after school.

A university in Lviv. Only 20% of Ukrainian students manage to enter higher educational institutions because the competition for some colleges can be as many as 20 applicants per available position.

EDUCATION

Eleven years of schooling are mandatory in Ukraine, so the secondary school system is a matter of concern for the government. Schools are state-run, and deviation from the standard curriculum, established by the Ministry of Education, is discouraged. The objective of general secondary school is to give younger students a good knowledge of the fundamentals of the arts and sciences, and to teach them how to use this knowledge practically.

Children start first grade at the age of six. Since there are no separate elementary, middle, and high schools, the division of classes is very informal, and all students from the first to 11th grades study in one building.

After the ninth grade, Ukrainian students have the option of going to a vocational or technical school rather than completing their secondary school education. Vocational and technical school programs can last anywhere from one year (if entered after graduation from secondary school) to three years (if entered after the ninth grade). Entering a college or a university is very competitive. Applicants are required to produce a secondary school certificate and to pass four entrance examinations.

MEDICINE

Ukraine has even more medical doctors per capita than the United States. Medical services in Ukraine are provided free of charge, however, the hospitals are outdated, underequipped, and in need of radical reforms. Working as a medical doctor in Ukraine is not as lucrative as it is in many countries, therefore many patients try to ensure that doctors take a personal interest in their case by offering them gifts and money in return for what they deem to be better treatment. In fact, this has almost become the rule. Most hospitals lack essential medicines and equipment, so experienced patients get their doctor's advice ahead of time and arrive at the hospital with their own supplies. There are a few private medical clinics that have emerged recently, and although the patients must pay for their treatment, the level of care is better.

Because the state does not have the resources to supply them, staples, such as pain relievers and disposable syringes are often not available in hospitals.

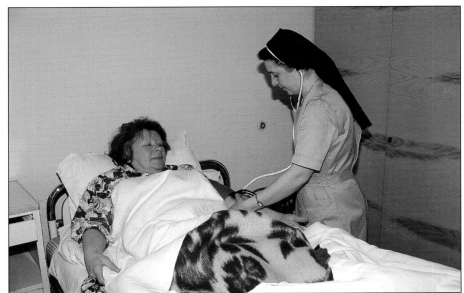

SOCIAL SERVICES

The official retirement age in Ukraine is 55 for women and 60 for men. Pensions are based on years of employment and salary averages during the final two years of service. The size of the pension is rarely more than 50% of the salary.

Since independence inflation, unstable prices, and general shortages have caused most pensioners to seek part-time jobs in order to survive. There are no private retirement homes, not only because the concept itself is unusual and very new, but also because the overwhelming majority of pensioners would not be able to afford the payments. State-run facilities are free, but they are only used as a last resort since the conditions are normally close to unbearable.

In addition to retirement homes, there are state-run orphanages and homes for the disabled, mostly kept running by the enthusiasm of the staff, and, more recently, by donations from newly-created private businesses.

State funds barely cover even the most basic of necessities for establishments such as this one for disabled children.

COMMUNICATION

"It is better to see once than to hear 100 times." This proverb characterizes the Ukrainian attitude towards communication. Ukrainians do not place a great deal of trust in telephones, faxes, or letters, therefore personal contact is always preferred. Meetings can be for a variety of purposes, either business, entertainment, or just to relax with friends.

Serious matters are never discussed over the telephone, not only because Ukrainians prefer to meet to discuss important issues, but also because telephone communication is unreliable and poorly-developed. Local calls rarely present a problem, but long distance calls are usually a challenge. Not only is it difficult to get through to the desired party, but the quality of the connection is often poor, and the line can be disconnected at any moment without warning. Telephones are not a fixed commodity in every household; many families do not have one at all. It is also very difficult to have a telephone installed since terminals are in short supply. More sophisticated methods of communication, like facsimile machines, can be found only in selected offices, and even then not on a regular basis, since many Ukrainian businesspeople do not see the need for fax machines at all. Electronic mail is only now making its way into Ukrainian communications. Regular mail is more in fashion, but it is not absolutely reliable.

Since many Ukrainians do not have private telephones in their homes, they rely on public telephones throughout the cities.

State-run stores like this one are rapidly becoming a thing of the past. Most Ukrainians have been forced to find new jobs since the conversion to privately run shops has eliminated the need for overstaffing.

EMPLOYMENT

According to the existing constitution, every Ukrainian citizen has the right to be employed. This fundamental right was protected by the USSR as well. Under the Soviet regime, state employment guaranteed a meager but stable salary. With the current economic crisis facing more and more state enterprises, employees are forced to look for additional part-time employment or to find an alternative source of income.

The transition from a state-run to a market economy has not been as smooth as some once anticipated. New private companies open and cease to exist almost weekly. Only a fraction of a percent of the newly registered private companies survive. Entrepreneurs expect that newly created independent businesses will produce immediate financial rewards, but most of them do not have the skills, knowledge, or persistence to make the companies succeed.

Unemployment rates are rising and military conversion processes have left an army of former military and police professionals without jobs. Highly trained specialists such as these cannot find other uses for their talents in the new Ukraine and many of them have resorted to violence and crime.

MOVING AROUND

"A car is not a luxury, but a means of transportation." This Soviet slogan never became a reality. Even today, cars are used mostly for special trips. Only one family out of 10 in Ukraine owns a car. Cars, even those made in the former Soviet Union, were always extremely expensive. In the 1980s, for example, a small popular car called a *Zhyguli* ("zhih-goo-LIH") cost anywhere between 8,000 to 12,000 rubles, with an average family income of around 4,500 rubles per year. Domestic cars were often not available, and foreign models were totally banned from the market.

The situation is approximately the same today. However, slowly the market has been opened to foreign cars, and today it is common to see used foreign cars on Ukrainian streets.

In Soviet Ukraine, gasoline and car repairs were very cheap. Today, most Ukrainians cannot afford to buy a car, or even maintain one they already own.

PUBLIC TRANSPORTATION

There are several different kinds of public transportation in Ukraine, all of them easily affordable to the average citizen. The most common forms of public transportation in most cities are buses, trolleybuses, and trams. In cities with populations over 1,000,000 as a rule there is always a subway. The subway, though as crowded as any other public transportation system in Ukraine, is efficient and runs on time. Electric trains take people from the suburbs and neighboring towns to the city's central railway station. For those who can afford them there are taxis, but in Kyiv during peak traffic hours it is usually faster to ride the subway than to take a taxi.

The life expectancy for the generation of Ukrainians born in 1993-1994 is 69 years. Men are expected to live on average for 64 years, and women for 74 years. These figures are among the lowest in Europe. Low life expectancy is attributed to living conditions, stress, and a polluted environment, including significant radioactive contamination caused by the Chornobyl disaster of 1986.

The only thing never in short supply were the parking spaces, available rather easily even in large city centers.

With some effort one can get train tickets on passenger trains that run throughout Ukraine, however there is usually a shortage of tickets particularly at holiday time when most people do their traveling.

Buses also travel to different cities in Ukraine but the state of the roads means trips are long and bumpy. Most Ukrainians only travel by bus when train tickets are not available. Airplane travel to international destinations is still only a dream for most Ukrainians.

RELIGION

ORTHODOX CHRISTIANITY is the dominant religion throughout Ukraine. In fact, over 35 million Ukrainians belong to the Orthodox Church. When Ukraine fell to the Russians in the 17th century, the Ukrainian Orthodox Church was absorbed into the Russian Orthodox Church. It has only been since 1990 that Ukrainians have begun to worship in their own language once more.

Other than slight differences in the procedures of the service, the two churches are nearly identical. Services are held in churches and cathedrals, although it is not easy to find an active church in Ukraine since many of them were converted to museums during the years of Soviet domination.

Currently there is a movement to restore the churches or build new ones if the damage is serious. Religious education, once limited to Kyiv and Odesa seminaries, is gaining popularity once more. In fact, the Orthodox Church is so active that its representatives can be seen in Parliament, local legislatures, electoral campaigns, and even in the army.

HISTORY OF CHRISTIANITY

Pre-Christian Ukrainians (the people of Kyivan Rus) were pagans. Their beliefs were conceived around the powers of nature, and gods were representations of nature's various elements: Wind, Rain, Frost, etc. In a country with long, cold winters, the most powerful god was the god of the Sun. If appropriately worshipped, the gods had the power to bring fertility, sunshine, wealth, and health. If defied, the gods sent drought, disease, and war. Reflections of these pagan beliefs can still be found in many Christian traditions.

71

Christianity made its way to Kyivan Rus almost immediately after the state was formed in the seventh century. Small groups of the population exposed to the influences of the Byzantine Empire adopted Christianity in the eighth and ninth centuries. The presence of Christian military men from Constantinople in 860 enhanced the spread of the religion and added to the number of believers.

It was only a century later, in 988, that Prince Volodymyr the Great adopted Christianity as the official religion for Kyivan Rus. The decision was dictated by the growing popularity of Christianity in Europe, and the need to integrate Kyivan Rus into the cultural, political, and economic life of the West. It was the Greek branch of Christianity that prevailed, and became the model on which Ukrainian and Russian Christianity were based for centuries to come.

The transition from pagan to Christian beliefs was not a smooth one. Chronicles tell of a crowd of Kyiv's inhabitants driven forcibly by soldiers to the Dnipro River and baptized there en masse. Statues of pagan gods were dismantled, burned, or thrown into the Dnipro. Many names in modern Kyiv reflect the events of those days. For example, the main street in Kyiv is *Hreschatyk* ("hreh-SCHAH-tik"), a derivation of "to cross," or to baptize, because it was the route the crowd was driven to the river by. Another part of the city is called *Holosiyivka* ("hoh-loh-SIH-iv-kah"), from the Ukrainian "to weep," because it was there that those who managed to escape from the forced baptism grieved their lost gods.

An image of Saturn, the god of seed or sowing. The festival of Saturn, Saturnalia is still celebrated in much of the Western world.

CHRISTIAN ARCHITECTURE

Constantinople sent missionaries to help Kyivan Rus establish Christianity. Byzantine priests taught Kyivan volunteers, who became the first Kyivan priests to continue the mission. Byzantine architects taught Kyivan masters to build Christian churches, which is when the beautiful onion-domed cathedrals first appeared in Kyiv, Novgorod, Volodymyr, and many other cities of Kyivan Rus. The first cathedrals were needed as soon as possible, so they were built of wood and covered with shingles. The typical feature in all Orthodox churches, ancient and modern, is the tripartite construction: a vestibule located in the west, a sanctuary in the east (the sanctuary is the part of the church where only the priest and his assistants are admitted), and the main area in between. The tradition of building bell towers separately from the churches originated with the necessity to avoid overloading the wooden structures. Later, architecture became more sophisticated, and brick and stone churches were built with several chapels surrounding the central room. A church was always constructed in the form of a cross, no matter how many parts it consisted of. Unlike many other churches, Ukrainian Orthodox churches do not have any pews, and those who come to pray either stand or kneel during services.

An old church made of wood and covered in shingles still stands in Lviv.

A Ukrainian Orthodox bishop giving a sermon.

WHAT IS ORTHODOX?

Just as the architecture of the church is meant to follow a certain pattern, so too are the church services. The method in which a church service progresses is the same as it has been for centuries. The sermon must always come from the holy books. The musical liturgy of the choir has been recorded for every occasion and cannot be selected randomly. This music is very specific and can only be heard in Orthodox churches. No musical instruments are allowed, and laughter, or even smiling, is prohibited—praying to God is a very serious matter. There are many small details of behavior absent in many other churches. For example, the correct way for Orthodox Christians to cross themselves, the correct way to light a candle (only from other candles, and never with a lighter or matches), the correct way to place one's hands (never behind one's back, and never in one's pockets), and many others. Ukrainian Orthodox women always wear kerchiefs over their heads when they attend church.

UKRAINIAN BAROQUE CHURCHES

Ukrainian baroque churches are built using a unique style of church architecture, sometimes called Kozak architecture, because it was used between the mid-17th and 18th centuries, the time of the most active Kozak movement. Ukrainian Kozak churches are a product of Byzantine and western European influences. Kozak churches were made of wood, and the wooden parts were connected without a single nail. Only a few of those churches have survived the misfortunes of time: floods, fires, and vandalism. They can be seen in central Ukraine, not far from Kyiv, Chernihiv, and Cherkasy.

OTHER RELIGIOUS DENOMINATIONS

It is difficult to know exactly how much of Ukraine's population has professed allegiance to the Ukrainian Orthodox Church, (also called the Ukrainian Autocephalous Church) and how many profess allegiance to the Russian Orthodox Church, but together they make up about 65% of the country's total population.

The Ukrainian Greek-Catholic Church (sometimes called the Uniate Church) has the second largest following in Ukraine. This denomination originated in 1596 for the benefit of Roman Catholic Poland, which dominated significant parts of Ukraine at the time. The Ukrainian Greek-Catholic Church follows the Eastern rites, while recognizing the leadership of the Pope in Rome. There are about five million faithful Greek-Catholics, most of whom live in the western part of Ukraine, which was ruled by the Poles for centuries.

Even with mass emigration in recent years, there are still more than 500,000 Jews in Ukraine. Several synagogues have opened their doors to serve Ukrainian Jews.

The Crimea has seen a resurgence of its first peoples, the Tatars. Many have returned from various places in the former Soviet Union, where they were once deported by the Stalin regime. Mosques and Islamic schools are once again becoming popular places for Muslims to practice their religion.

The current Ukrainian government is tolerant to all kinds of religious activities provided they bring no harm to society.

KYIVO-PECHERSKA LAVRA (THE CAVE MONASTERY)

Kyivo-Pecherska Lavra ("KIH-ih-voh peh-CHER-skah LAH-vrah") is the conclave of the oldest monastery in Ukraine, built at the dawn of the Christian era in Kyivan Rus. "Lavra" is a term reserved for monasteries of the highest importance under the direct jurisdiction of the Patriarch. Besides Kyivo-Pecherska, only one other monastery in western Ukraine has gained the status of lavra. Just

as Mecca is a sacred place for Muslims to visit at least once in their lifetime, Kyivo-Pecherska Lavra in Kyiv has become a sacred place for all Orthodox Christians. The monastery consists of numerous churches, a huge bell tower, dormitories, a maze of caves, underground rooms, and communication corridors. The original caves were excavated in the 11th century and served not only as a place to hide from invaders, but also as a place to meditate in solitude, isolated from the cruelty of the outside world.

RELIGION TODAY

There were about 80,000 Orthodox churches in the Russian Empire before the Revolution of 1917, of which less than 8,000 remained by 1980.

"They all have hidden crosses on their foreheads," an American once concluded about Ukrainians after a long term visit to Ukraine. This observation is fairly accurate considering the lengths the Communist regime went to to discourage religion. At universities, besides an enormous number of ideological subjects, there was also a mandatory course on "scientific atheism." The subject was designed to prove that there was no God. Anyone who wanted to reach success in their career was forced to pronounce themselves an atheist. Religion was seen as the most serious obstacle to building Communism.

Things have changed since then, and the "cross on the forehead" no longer needs to be hidden. Religion has returned to homes and neighborhoods in the form of icons and restored churches. In 1988, even before Ukraine's official independence, Kyiv attracted thousands of visitors for the celebration of the Millennium of Christianity in Rus at Kyivo-Pecherska Lavra, despite the fact that at the time it was still labeled a museum.

Though Ukraine still has a long way to go to re-establish pre-revolutionary conditions, the liberation of religion in Ukraine has attracted numerous preachers, missionaries, and prophets from all over the world.

For the younger generation the return to religion has become a popular trend. What was once considered old fashioned behavior and disapproved of by the Communist youth, is today not only condoned, it has been taken up by droves of young Ukrainians.

WITCHCRAFT, BLACK AND WHITE MAGIC

There are many religious superstitions in Ukraine that are a fusion of pagan and Christian beliefs. Speaking with somebody while standing in the threshold, a black cat crossing one's path, whistling inside the house—these and many others are said to bring bad luck. Many Ukrainians believe in black magic, and its opposing force, white magic. Witches are said to have the power to prevent crops from growing, or kill livestock. The witch's curse is also believed to drive its victim to the grave by inexplicable disease or a strange accident. In Ukrainian folk tales, though, a brave Kozak always overcame the curses, devil's temptations, and all kinds of witchcraft by his strong faith, keen wits, and optimism.

LANGUAGE

UKRAINIAN LANGUAGE HAS SUFFERED GREATLY from the influence of the Russian language. Though mutual influence is natural and unavoidable in border areas, Russian was the official language for the entire Union of Soviet Socialist Republics. This meant that all business correspondence, official communication, and printed newspapers were in Russian. Ukrainians demanded bilingual passports, licenses, and certificates, however they met with little success. National radio stations and television channels were broadcast solely in Russian, and although the Ukrainian mass media was permitted to operate, it was much less influential and pervasive than its Russian counterpart.

Attempts to russify the nation were not limited to language, but language, as a crucial emblem of national spirit, was an important loss. After the fall of the Soviet Union, the revival of the Ukrainian language was one of the first reforms passed by Ukrainian Parliament.

However, the problem of language was not that easy a matter to solve seeing as Ukraine is populated by 15 million Russians, and many Ukrainians speak better Russian than Ukrainian, having been taught Russian in school. In fact, Russian and Ukrainian are very closely related, with a 60% shared word-stock, but for some it is a matter of national pride more than an issue of literacy. One of the demands of striking miners in eastern Ukraine was to make Russian the second official language.

Opposite: **A movie poster in Chernyvtsi center, western Ukraine.**

Below: **The Kozaks, painted on the wall behind this boy, were the protectors of the Ukrainian language. In the Kozak settlements, men, women, and children were taught to read and write.**

UKRAINIAN

Ukrainian belongs to the large family of Indo-European languages, along with English, Spanish, and many other languages. At the same time, Ukrainian also belongs to the Slavic group, along with Polish, Bulgarian, and Russian, while English is part of the Germanic group, along with German and Dutch. Therefore, although the Ukrainian and English languages are related, their kinship is rather a distant one.

The relationship, however, is evident in certain words, for example, two and three in English are *dva* ("de-VA") and *try* ("TRY") in Ukrainian, the English word beat is *byty* ("BIT-tea")in Ukrainian, and water translates as *voda* ("VO-da"). There are many other words that only comparative linguistics can identify as being related. In some cases it is not clear whether a word has the same origin or it was just borrowed from another language (compare the English word hut with the Ukrainian *khata*, "CA-ta," meaning in both languages approximately the same thing). There are very few words in the English language borrowed from the Ukrainian, but there are many words used in Ukrainian that are borrowed from English. Words representing specific actvities or items originating in foreign culture in the last century, such as *jazz, jeans, computer, rock-'n-roll,* have been adopted without any changes. However, there are also words that sound almost identical but mean quite different things, to the confusion of inexperienced translators. For example, the Ukrainian *mahazyn* ("ma-ha-ZEEN") means store, not magazine.

A road sign written in Ukrainian. It has only been since independence that Ukrainian has come back into official use.

WRITTEN UKRAINIAN

At the end of the 11th century, the Slavic languages began to exhibit distinct differences. This is usually explained by migration and cultural influence from neighboring countries. Today, it is easy to tell that Russian was influenced by the Scandinavian languages and Tatar, while Ukrainian, preserving its Old Slavonic roots, adopted many words from Poland, Russia, and Austria.

The written Ukrainian language originated in the ninth century, when the Byzantine missionaries, St. Cyril and St. Methodius, created an alphabet based on Greek and Hebrew letters. This system of characters is called the Cyrillic alphabet, after St. Cyril. The Cyrillic alphabet, used by the brothers to translate the Bible into the Slavic language, is used today (with some variations) by Ukrainians, Russians, Belarussians, Bulgarians, and other Slavic nations.

The Ukrainian alphabet has 33 letters. One letter, the soft sign, does not have its own sound, but makes the preceding consonant "soft," thus changing its pronunciation.

A book bazaar in Mariupol, the Donetsk region. Ukrainians take great pride in their home libraries and government education laws mean that nearly 100% of Ukrainians are literate.

There are two features of Ukrainian which make it easy for the English speaker to learn: the letters are pronounced exactly the way they are pronounced in the alphabet, regardless of the accented or unaccented position in the word, and the structure of the sentence is more flexible than in English.

THE MASS MEDIA IN UKRAINE

In a famous Ukrainian joke, a member of the inspection committee asks a randomly-selected person in the streets of Kyiv: "Do you have everything that you need? —Yes. —Can you buy everything in state stores? —Sure. —Do you read newspapers? —Of course, how else would I know that I have everything?"

The joke illustrates the ridiculous difference between what was written in newspapers and the actual situation in Ukraine before independence. All mass media was state-owned and state-supported. Reporters' material was thoroughly censored by editors, who were appointed to their

Reading the newspaper in a park in Kyiv.

83

There are three Ukrainian greetings, depending on the time of day. Dobryy ranok (*"DOH-brii RAH-nok"), Good Morning;* Dobryy den (*"DOH-brii DEN'"), Good Afternoon;* Dobryy vechir (*"DOH-brii VEH-chir"), Good Evening.*

positions and strictly supervised by the Communist Party committee. No matter what happened in the country, news was always optimistic. The most one could find out about a plane crash, if anything at all, was something like "there were victims." A disaster the size of the Chornobyl nuclear power plant explosion was not even mentioned in the press. To keep control over such powerful mass media as television and radio, the central leadership prevented the development of local television stations. Thus, there were only two television channels from Moscow, and one or two from Kyiv available in Ukraine. Crammed with propaganda, the national channels' advantage was the complete absence of commercial advertising. The same was true for radio.

The development of private electronic mass media has been slowed by delays in the Law on Television and Radio Broadcasting, which was legislated by Parliament in 1994. The constant changes in the State Committee on Television and Radio Broadcasting have caused bureaucratic delays as well. According to new laws, priority will be given to stations promoting Ukrainian culture and language. The law requires all private television and radio stations to program a minimum of 50% domestic content, as opposed to devoting air time to powerful satellite services, such as Voice of America, or the BBC.

Freedom of the press and electronic mass media is guaranteed by the Ukrainian Constitution, a guarantee which produced unexpected results. As thousands of newly-created printed newspapers appeared on the market (private radio and television developed more slowly), the standard and quality fell below what was previously judged as normal.

Television and radio have introduced massive commercial advertising into every available minute. Commercials are imported from the West and translated into Ukrainian.

DIALECTS AND NON-VERBAL COMMUNICATION

Some of the peculiarities in pronunciation and vocabulary make it easy to distinguish a person from the Poltava area in central Ukraine from one in western Ukraine, and a person from the south from one who lives in the east. Subjected to continuous invasions and numerous outside influences, Ukrainians in these areas have developed very distinctive dialects. Of course, not everyone in these regions uses the same patterns, and there is a standard Ukrainian language used by the media and taught in schools, so there are generally few problems of miscommunication.

A teacher reading to children in a day care center. Children in Ukraine are admitted to child-care centers when they are less than one year old, so they learn to communicate with people outside the family when they are very young.

Gestures and instinctive reactions also figure prominently in communication. Ukrainians use their hands, movements of the head, and facial expressions to strengthen the meaning of their words. Some gestures are common outside Ukraine as well, for example, the slight nodding of one's head while listening to the conversation (meaning "I comprehend and agree"); shaking one's head from left to right (meaning "I disagree"); or clapping one's hands (signifying approval and encouragement). Whistling during concerts and performances is a sign of disapproval in Ukraine.

FORMS OF ADDRESS

The terms Mr. and Mrs. in Ukraine were supplanted 75 years ago by the genderless "comrade." The explanation was that Mr. and Mrs. were used to address people in a superior position, while under Communism everyone is meant to be equal. Today the traditional *pan* ("pahn") for Mr., *pani* ("PAH-nih") for Mrs., and *panna* ("PAH-nah") for Miss are gradually replacing comrade, however, which form of address is the appropriate one is temporarily a puzzle for Ukrainians, who, to avoid any bias, very often do not use any address at all in letters other than the name.

There are two ways to say "you" in Ukrainian: the formal *vy* and the informal *ty*. The second, as a rule, is used when people address each other by their first names, which does not happen as readily in Ukraine as it does in North America. It is rude to call someone by their last name or their first name if it is the first meeting. The first name in combination with the patronymic name is the best approach. For example, Ivan Mykolayovych is the appropriate way to address a man, or Tetyana Petrivna for a woman.

PROVERBS IN COMPARISON

Every country in the world uses proverbs to demonstrate life's lessons. A comparison of proverbs in Ukrainian and English shows the similarities that abound across borders.

Ukrainian: *Ridna zemlya i v zhmeni myla.* (Native soil is dear even if it is only a handful.)
English: East or West, home is best.
Ukrainian: *Nasha syla—sim'ya yedyna.* (Our strength is in the united family.)
English: United we stand, divided we fall.
Ukrainian: *Khto rano posiye, toy rano y pozhne.* (Those who plant early will harvest early.)
English: The early bird catches the worm.
Ukrainian: *Iz vohniu ta v polum'ya.* (Out of the flames into the fire.)
English: Out of the frying pan and into the fire.

TATAR

The Tatar language is part of the northwestern or Kipchak Turkic language group, including Kirgiz, Kazakh, Kara-Kalpak, Nogay, Kumyk, Bashkir, Karaim, Karachay, and Balkar. The development of a distinct Turkic language began in the eighth century in Inner Asia. Arabic script was generally used by all Turkic peoples until the early 1920s, when Latin script was adopted by the Turkic peoples of the USSR. After 1939, Latin script was almost completely replaced in the USSR by modern forms of the Cyrillic alphabet. The Arabic alphabet is still used by Turkic peoples living in China and the Arab countries.

Monument in Lviv to the first book printer, Ivan Fiodorov.

One of the most distinctive features of Turkic languages is vowel harmony. There are two kinds of vowels, front vowels produced at the front of the mouth (e, i, ö, ü), and back vowels produced at the back of the mouth (a, o, u). Vowel harmony has been broken down in some languages, but purely Turkic words contain either all front or all back vowels. Word formation is governed by agglutination, which is the use of suffixes to express grammatical concepts rather than independent words. For example, the word *evlerimde* (in my house), is composed of *ev* (house), *ler* (plural suffix), *im* (possessive suffix of first person singular), *de* (location suffix in).

ARTS

TWO MAIN FORCES drove the development of art in Ukraine: service to God, and the desire to express emotion through decoration and depiction of the environment. Popular motifs were derived from the various stages in Ukraine's history. From the mysterious Trypillian culture came the spiral, repeated again and again as a symbol of the ongoing creation of life; eggs painted with swastikas were an expression of the ancient Sanskrit symbol of never-ending progress; circles represented the Sun, the most important of the pagan gods; crosses were embroidered in cloth to guard and protect the name of the Savior. Foreign conquerors attempted to prevent these art forms, but the oppression only strengthened the folk art movement as an expression of national identity.

Opposite: **Ukrainian Easter eggs painted in the pysanka style.**

Below: **An Annunciation icon painted in a church in Lviv.**

RELIGIOUS ICONS

Service to God in art is characterized best of all by the variety of church icons. To make these icons a wooden plate was sanded down until the surface was clean and smooth for painting. The paints were made from a base of egg yokes and other natural ingredients, but the recipe was lost long ago. The oldest surviving icons were painted in the 11th century, depicting events in the Bible and saints in Eastern Orthodox history. The oldest paintings can be seen at Kyiv's St. Sofia Cathedral.

The craft of the *bohomaz* ("boh-hoh-MAHZ"), as the artists were called, was well respected, but contrary to popular belief, the artists were not. In fact, very often they were serfs working for a landlord who would allow them to contract work with churches and give them only a small share of the payment.

Intricately embroidered patterns are a trademark of Ukrainian art.

EMBROIDERY

For hundreds of years, Ukrainian women have dedicated long winter nights to weaving, embroidering, and arranging complicated bead designs on their clothing. Traditionally, mothers and their daughters embroidered a shirt, handkerchief, or tobacco pouch for their husbands, sons, or sweethearts. Floral designs were embroidered on towels and napkins that were hung in the kitchen and throughout the house. Embroidery can also be found in the interior of churches.

Embroidery is a long process that demands time and patience. Different parts of the country have their own particular patterns, but black and red thread against a white background are the prevailing colors throughout the country.

"Red for love, black for sorrow." Red and black are traditional colors in many fields of Ukrainian art, representing life's two polarities.

POTTERY

While initially pottery was a practical way of equipping the kitchen with the necessary utensils, later it grew into an art form. Recently, traditional pottery is regaining popularity in Ukraine. Folk art items are beginning to appear in Ukrainian homes to replace standard commercial goods. There are large deposits of many varieties of clays throughout Ukraine, which has been a major factor in the growth and development of this art form.

EASTER EGGS

The art of decorating eggs in the spring has become associated with Easter over the years, but this art form existed long before Christianity came to Ukraine. In many countries around the world, spring is a celebration of new life, and Ukrainians believe there is a great power in the new life embodied in an egg. Ancient legends tell of a giant egg from which the universe emerged. Eggs were believed to have the power to heal, protect, and to bring good luck and wealth. Such beliefs are the reason behind the tradition of keeping a plateful of decorated eggs in the home.

After the introduction of Christianity to Ukraine, the art of egg decorating continued to develop. Today there are two types of decorated Easter eggs. The simpler one, called *krashanka* ("KRAH-shahn-kah"), is an edible boiled egg painted with one bright color (*kraska,* "KRAHS-kah" is the root word, from the Slavic for "paint"). The more detailed *pysanka* ("PIH-sahn-kah"), is a raw egg painted with various colors and designs and kept in the house as decoration. The difference can be most clearly seen in the root word *pysaty* ("pih-SAH-tih"), meaning "to write."

The long, careful procedure used when making pysanka eggs is one of the things that makes them so beautiful. The design, determined ahead of time, is drawn in wax on the surface of the

It is a Ukrainian tradition to keep Easter eggs in the house throughout the year to ward off evil.

Petrykivka *("pet-rih-KIV-kah") is a small town in Ukraine that has become famous both in Ukraine and outside for its distinctive style of painting. The Petrykivka style is a combination of flowers and historical motifs. The design can be seen on Easter eggs, wooden plates, spoons, cutting boards, or wall paintings.*

egg. Then, the egg is dipped in different colored dyes, from brightest to darkest, with new wax being applied between dippings. The wax pattern seals the color, so the artist must keep the image of the final design in mind at all times—it is impossible to "rewrite" anything on the surface of the egg. Before the final step, when the wax is heated and wiped from the egg, the design cannot be seen. In fact, the egg looks most unattractive. This makes the impression even stronger when the miracle of the artist's creation suddenly appears the moment the wax is removed.

Traditionally, the dyes were made of various herbs and plants, including sunflower seeds, walnuts, buckwheat husks, moss, and birch leaves. Today, the dyes can be bought as powder and mixed when necessary. The same is true for the *kistka* ("KIST-kah"), or stylus, the tool used for drawing the wax pattern. In the old days, the stylus had to be filled with wax and warmed by the flame of a candle every minute to ensure that the wax did not cool. Today, there are electric styluses of various sizes that, when plugged in, keep the temperature regulated so the wax is always hot.

MUSIC

Ukrainian is a very melodious language. But the "sing song" sound of the language only partially explains why Ukrainians like to sing so much. Music is inevitably a part of any party or get together, used to express both joy and sorrow.

Ukrainian music was developed on the basis of folk songs, many of them composed and spread by *kobzars* ("kob-ZAHR"), bards who traveled from town to town performing their music. The name kobzar was derived from the name of the musical instrument they used to accompany their songs. The kobza is an ancient Ukrainian instrument (very much like a round lute with three or four strings), a predecessor of the *bandura*

A Ukrainian music group busking on the street.

("bahn-DOO-rah"), another stringed musical instrument. The bandura, which is asymmetrical in shape and contains up to 60 strings, became popular in the 17th century. In the Carpathian Mountains one can also play the *trembita* ("trem-BEE-tah"), a wind instrument with a profoundly mournful sound. Made in the shape of a cylindrical tube, trembitas can be as long as 10 feet (3 m).

Unlike in other countries, Ukrainian folk music has never merged with popular music. There have been several attempts in recent years to create a uniquely Ukrainian rock-'n-roll, but it has never found much of a following.

Some of the most famous Ukrainian folk singers are Nina Matviyenko, Raisa Kyrychenko, and Anatoliy Solov'yanenko. Mykola Lysenko, a passionate promoter of Ukrainian music and Mykola Leontovych, the author of the world-famous *Carol of the Bells*, are other well-known Ukrainian musicians.

DANCE

Dance, as a form of art or simply as entertainment, is very popular in Ukraine. Folk dances vary in style, depending on the region. In the west, group dances comprised of both men and women are popular. The ritual meaning of the dances has been forgotten, and today they are usually danced to commemorate important events (weddings, in particular) and to entertain the public.

What is known to the world as Kozak dancing indeed originated with the Kozaks of the 16th century, but not as a dance at all. The movements were part of a regime of calisthenics to keep the Kozaks fit for battles. It was not until much later that it was transformed into a group dance with leaps, rapid movements, and comic improvisations. This dance is called the *hopak* ("hoh-PAHK"), and it can be performed only by very well trained artists. One of the best professional groups in Ukraine is the Hopak Kyiv Dance Troop.

LITERATURE, FILM, AND THEATER

Ukrainian writers and poets (with the possible exception of Taras Shevchenko) are not generally known internationally. This is largely due to the suppression of Ukrainian culture in the 18th and 19th centuries. Literature was the most powerful instrument in an ongoing battle to promote Ukrainian nationalism. Ukrainians remember with gratitude such names as Ivan Franko, Yuriy Kotsubynskyy, Marko Vovchok, and many others. When it was forbidden to write in Ukrainian, these were the few who continued to do so despite the consequences. Other Ukrainian writers were forced to write in Russian, but most never forgot their roots.

Ukrainian theater never reached a golden age, however, Mykola Lysenko, talented composer and author of the historical opera *Taras Bulba,* and Semen Hulak-Artemovskyy, composer of *The Kozak Beyond the Danube,* are two well-known Ukrainians whose operas are still performed in theaters throughout Ukraine.

Ukraine has three major film studios in Kyiv, Odesa, and Kharkiv. One of the most prominent movie-makers, Oleksandr Dovzhenko (Kyiv film studio was named for him), was blamed by the Soviets for the promotion of Ukrainian nationalism. The Ukrainian film industry has many gifted and popular actors, who have been recognized within the former USSR and internationally.

During the years of Soviet domination, Ukrainian was not forbidden, but no literature directed at the development of Ukrainian culture was tolerated. Since independence, the government has given priority to the development of Ukrainian literature.

The famous Opera House in Odesa.

LEISURE

THE SWITCH FROM LABOR to leisure in Ukraine is not as planned or natural as it is in other countries. Ukrainians prefer to work as hard as possible to complete a task in one attempt, no matter how long it takes, in order to have their leisure completely unshadowed by thoughts of unfinished work.

There are a variety of different ways for Ukrainians to spend their free time. Picnics are a popular way to combine the relaxation of eating, drinking, singing, and getting some fresh air. Movies, plays, and ballet are a great weekend activity if tickets are available.

Unfortunately weekends are usually the only time for people to take care of chores at home. That is why for many people painting, gardening, cleaning, and general household repairs have become leisure activities.

Opposite: **Ice-fishing is one of the most popular winter pastimes in Ukraine.**

Left: **The rolling hills of central and western Ukraine make for challenging hiking.**

A festive family dinner.

AT HOME

There are people in Ukraine who could easily qualify as "couch potatoes," with only one difference—it is not so much that they are chained to the couch, but that they have a love of the home in general. "Let's get together on Saturday, our place," is a typical weekend invitation which is extended spontaneously to a friend during a telephone conversation on Friday. The invitation is usually accepted or rejected on the spot. For Ukrainians, eating is a form of leisure. Having a meal is not just a way to satisfy one's hunger, it is also a time to chat with friends and family about the day's events or the political situation. Since extended families are often in close contact, relatives may get together for dinner once or twice a week. In cases like these, the whole family pitches in to help with the food arrangements.

TELEVISION AND NEWSPAPERS

Spending an evening in front of the television has become routine leisure for many Ukrainian families. However, there are no home shopping networks, no cable television, and no instant weather reports. In fact, the number of channels even in Kyiv is limited to five or six, and a 25-inch television is considered a gigantic model. But, large or small, televisions have become an essential commodity for nearly every Ukrainian family. Since there are no TV-guides, local and national newspapers compete to publish programming schedules because it is a sure way to increase circulation. Recently, with international channels becoming available and, in some cases one or two specialized cable channels, parents have started to become concerned about their children's leisure time because television competes with friends, homework, and reading.

Today, newspapers provide as much variety in entertainment as television does. There are dozens of different editions dedicated to a wide variety of topics, from politics to sports to the erotic.

Yachting is a popular pastime for Ukrainians, particularly in the summer.

SPORTS

Sports complexes can be found in every large city in Ukraine. These complexes usually house a swimming pool, and facilities for aerobics, boxing, and team games. For students there are sports academies, or their own secondary school facilities. But if nothing is available, just a flat grassy surface somewhere in the park will do.

Adults are also taking part in amateur sports competitions. The most popular amateur sports are soccer, basketball,

volleyball, hockey, and boxing. Tennis is slowly making its way to Ukraine, and more recently martial arts, such as *karate* and *kung fu*. Golfers will be disappointed, however, as there are still no golf courses in Ukraine.

Ukrainian athletes were some of the strongest members of the Soviet Olympic teams. Some of these athletes have gained worldwide recognition, such as pole-vaulter Serhiy Bubka, gymnasts Tetiana Hutsul and Hryhory Misyutin, and figure skaters Oksana Baiul and Viktor Petrenko, to name a few. Ukraine participated as an independent nation for the first time in the 1996 Atlanta Olympics (in 1992 Ukraine participated as a member of the Commonwealth of Independent States), and took nine gold medals, two silver medals, and 12 bronze medals, finishing the games in ninth place.

A boy and his bicycle near the village of Spac.

Soccer is the national sport of Ukraine, however, to date it is exclusively a men's sport. There are many young Ukrainian boys who dream of becoming famous soccer players on the Kyiv *Dynamo*. On the day of the final game in a championship match, all activity comes to a halt while fans watch the action on TV, or listen to the coverage on the radio.

Cycling can also be considered a popular pastime. For many people living in towns, bicycles are a means of transportation, especially appreciated in the days of fuel shortages. More serious cyclists participate in organized bicycle marathons. Though there are few special bicycle paths and trails, the traffic in Ukraine is fairly light, which makes cycling on the city streets a safe and convenient way to travel and get some exercise at the same time.

There is a traditional marathon that takes place in Odesa every year, dedicated to the anniversary of the city's liberation from Nazi occupation during World War II. The participants follow a route around the city called the *Circle of Glory*, where the monuments to the defenders of the city are located. People of all age groups take part in marathons like this one.

TRAVEL

Vacation time begins as soon as the weather is warm enough, usually the middle of May until the middle of August. Some Ukrainians plan their vacations ahead of time by booking a tour package through a travel agency. Other people take what are called "wild" vacations in Ukraine, meaning they drive to their chosen destination, pitch a tent, and cook their food over a campfire. The absence of laws for private land ownership make trips like these possible, but local governments in towns by the seaside do their best to keep the hordes of "wild" tourists to a minimum.

The beach in Simeiz, a Crimean health resort.

Sunbathing at a Black Sea resort.

International destinations have long been the dream of many Ukrainian travelers. In the past, because of the political situation and the lack of hard currency, these trips were destined to remain dreams. Today, Ukrainians are free to travel the world, but for the majority of the population, international travel is still too costly. Since independence, however, a large number of émigrés have returned to visit their relatives.

REST HOMES AND SANATORIUMS

There are two types of facilities designed specifically for relaxation, leisure and health restoration—rest homes and sanatoriums. Although neither are equipped to deal with specialized health problems, one can expect to see medical personnel milling around to make guests feel more comfortable.

Most guests stay for a period of three weeks and are treated to comfortable rooms, good food and entertainment, and therapeutic treatment on a daily basis by trained specialists. Rest homes and sanatoriums are generally located in quiet, picturesque places away from the hubbub of large cities. Formerly subsidized by state funds, the facilities were quite affordable for many Ukrainians, however, since the introduction of the self-financing system, many of them have become rather expensive.

There are many popular resorts on the Ukrainian part of the Black Sea and on shores of the Sea of Azov. The largest is Odesa, where the population of one million more than doubles during the summer months. The Crimea has Yalta, Feodosiya, Alushta, and all the seashore in between for spas, hotels, and beautiful beaches. Several places on the Sea of Azov with its shallow warm waters offer good accommodation as well.

Having lunch on a hike in the Carpathian Mountains in western Ukraine.

ALONE WITH NATURE

Some people's idea of a perfect vacation is to escape the city crowds and surround themselves with nature. Though Ukraine is a densely populated country, it is still possible to find an isolated spot on the bank of a river or lake to fish, camp, and swim.

Others desire something more adventurous and during the summer months, white water rafting down Ukraine's major rivers is a thrilling ride. In June, July, or August, elaborate rafts with single travelers or whole families can be seen on the Dnister, Dnipro, or Privdennyy Bug rivers.

If one prefers to have a winter vacation, there are many resort areas, especially in the Carpathian Mountains. For those interested in skiing, there is no better place than Yaremcha in western Ukraine, renowned for its beauty, delicious food, and spas, not to mention the excellent ski slopes.

FESTIVALS

THERE ARE TWO TYPES of holidays in Ukraine—religious and political. In the past, political holidays were celebrated on the anniversaries of the Revolution of 1917, on the day when the latest variant of the constitution was adopted, and on May 1st as an expression of the solidarity of the working classes of the world. Religious holidays were not officially celebrated at all, but unofficially people observed them the way their ancestors had done for centuries. The holidays were found on the church calendar, issued by the Ukrainian Orthodox Patriarch's office every year.

All the changes in the political, economic, and cultural life of Ukrainians have been reflected in their holidays. Holidays with political significance to the former USSR are generally not celebrated. Religious festivals have taken their place. All in all, independence has meant that there are more red figures (indicating days off) on the calendar.

The 1st of May used to be celebrated as the International Day of Workers' Solidarity. In the USSR there were "demonstrations of solidarity" on the 1st of May. Today, the political meaning of the 1st of May is lost, and instead people simply celebrate the coming of spring.

Opposite: **Two women dressed in traditional Ukrainian festival dress.**

Left: **A Ukrainian folk festival.**

REMEMBERING THE WAR

Many people are puzzled when they see the size of World War II memorials in Ukraine. One in Kyiv, for example, is larger than the famous Cave Monastery, and the central monument, a woman holding a sword symbolizing the country ready to defend itself, is almost as tall as the tallest bell tower in the monastery. Ukrainians may differ on the subject of investment in war memorials, but eight million Ukrainians died in World War II, a tragedy which is shared by virtually every family in the country.

The Defence of the Motherland Monument in Kyiv.

THE AFGHANISTAN WAR

When the Soviet Union entered Afghanistan in 1979, an official report was issued stating that the USSR intended to provide help to a group of struggling Afghans at their request. Nobody in the USSR expected the involvement to grow into a full-scale war that would last more than 10 years. Beginning in 1980, service in Afghanistan became a mandatory part of "real war" training for young military professionals, from which many returned in zinc coffins. There was no choice for the 18-year-old boys drafted for compulsory army service. Tens of thousands died in Afghanistan, and hundreds of thousands returned with physical and mental scars. The veterans from Afghanistan in Ukraine formed what is called "the lost generation." When the young soldiers finally came home, they found it extremely difficult to readjust to life in a peaceful environment.

Victory Day, the 9th of May, is a tribute to the countless soldiers who gave their lives defending Ukraine. It is also an anti-war holiday, a reminder of the atrocities of war. Flowers are brought to the memorials, which can be found in every city and village in Ukraine. Veterans wear their decorations and gather together to share their memories. Once only the veterans of the Soviet Army took to the streets on this day, but since independence veterans of the Ukrainian Liberation Army (who fought both the German and Soviet armies in western Ukraine) freely celebrate Victory Day. Recently, younger people in uniforms can be seen gathering with the Liberation Army veterans and the veterans of World War II. These are the veterans of the war in Afghanistan.

INTERNATIONAL WOMEN'S DAY

The 8th of March is a holiday for all women, mothers first and foremost. The holiday was established by a German Communist Party Leader named Clara Zetkin to commemorate the struggle for women's rights. Over the years it has lost much of its political meaning, and today it is comparable to Mother's Day in other countries. Husbands, boyfriends, fathers, and sons do their best to make this day as enjoyable as possible for women. Most families try to do something special for mother by preparing a special dinner, making a card, or bringing home flowers. International Women's Day is a national holiday in Ukraine.

Children dressed and ready to celebrate Christmas.

CHRISTMAS

Ukrainians celebrate Christmas on the 7th of January, the date of Christ's birth according to the Eastern Orthodox calendar. On Christmas Eve, churches hold special services based on ancient rituals. The priests dress in festive garments of silver and gold, and the choir performs anthems. After the service, family members gather at someone's home for a festive dinner. The tradition of Christmas carolling is alive and well in Ukraine, and long before Christmas Eve people make sure there are enough cookies, candies, and small coins for all the carollers. The pre-Revolutionary tradition was to present the carollers with food (sausages and bread) and

Kolach ("KO-latch") is special bread baked for Christmas. The candle represents Jesus Christ, light of the world.

a shot of *horilka* ("hoh-RIL-kah"), Ukrainian vodka. Greetings from the visiting group can be in the form of a short poem, or a song wishing household members happiness and health. On these days it is difficult to believe that it was only a few years ago that all religious holidays were officially prohibited. Older people still remember the circles of activists who surrounded churches on Christmas Eve to prevent children (who were members of the *Young Communist League*) from watching the service.

EASTER

Another important religious holiday is Easter. Preparations for the holiday begin 40 days before Easter Sunday, on Ash Wednesday. The Lenten season is rather strict—the faithful do not eat meat or animal fat for 40 days, and avoid cheese and oils seven days before Easter Sunday. Everything must be cleaned and decorated for Easter, including the interior and exterior of the home. There are several solemn pre-Easter church services, with the culmination on Easter Sunday. Each family brings a basket of foods to the church on Sunday morning to be blessed with holy water by the priest. After the food has been blessed, everyone goes home to break the fast. On Easter Sunday it is customary to greet people with the words "Christ is Risen" to which they answer, "He is Risen indeed!"

Priests blessing baskets of food. Easter is a time to forgive sins and forget anger.

NEW YEAR

A New Year's procession with flowers and a decorated New Year's tree travels from house to house to wish people a Happy New Year.

During the years when celebrating Christmas was prohibited, New Year became a very important holiday. In fact, today New Year is probably considered the biggest holiday of the year. Ukrainians put up New Year trees, which they decorate with all kinds of ornaments. The trees came to be known as New Year's trees because although they are decorated to celebrate Christmas, they are brought to the house a few days before the New Year, and stand until the 13th of January. The 13th of January is a special day for some Ukrainians who still celebrate "Old New Year," the start of the new year according to the old calendar, abolished long ago by Peter the Great.

New Year is a time for family reunions, and people travel long distances in order to gather with their relatives at this time of year. New Year is symbolic of the beginning of a new and better life, and even the boldest wishes are believed to come true on this day.

New Year's Eve is full of laughter and entertainment, eating, drinking, dancing, and playing games. Many people celebrate throughout the night, and do not go to bed at all.

A Catholic Palm Sunday procession through the streets of Lviv.

OTHER HOLIDAYS

Palm Sunday is the first day of Holy Week and the Sunday before Easter. In Ukraine, the Palm Sunday procession travels from the church where the palms are blessed to the church where the liturgies are sung.

A relatively new tradition is to celebrate the Day of the City. For some of the newer cities, like Odesa, which celebrated its bicentennial in 1994, it is easy to trace the day of its foundation. For other cities, people must estimate. For example, it is estimated that Kyiv is 1,500 years old. Whether or not the date is correct, everyone enjoys the colorful annual festivals.

THE HOLIDAY OF TRINITY

Although it is not a day off, Trinity is the most important religious holiday after Christmas and Easter. It is celebrated in June, when the trees are green and beautiful, and for this reason it is also called "the green holiday." According to the scriptures, the Holy Spirit appeared before the Apostles on the 50th day after Jesus Christ's resurrection and granted them the ability to speak all the world's languages in order to preach the world over.

People visit each other on this day and enjoy festive meals. The interiors of homes are decorated with fresh green grass and tree branches, symbolizing the flourishing of life.

FOOD

FOOD HAS ALWAYS HELD SPECIAL MEANING for the people of the breadbasket of Europe. Ukrainians take eating very seriously, and, particularly when there is a guest in the house, the preparation of meals requires a special effort. It is not only the flavor of the food which is important, it is the whole sensation of the meal, from the table setting, to the crockery, to the complimentary colors of the food.

Like many other countries in the world, Ukraine has experienced food shortages, and the famine which ravaged the land in the 1930s is still fresh in the minds of many. The rich black soil has provided Ukraine with the means to feed herself, and all Ukrainians are thankful for this.

Opposite: **Potatoes are a staple in the Ukrainian diet.**

Below: **Selling broad beans and carrots in a western Ukrainian market.**

FRUITS AND VEGETABLES

There has never been an abundance of fruit in Ukraine. However, apples, cherries, plums, and other fruits grown in temperate climates are readily available. The same is true of vegetables—many Ukrainians have never heard of avocados, parsnips, or sweet potatoes, to say nothing of the exotic leeks. Due to the trade regulations of the "iron curtain," imported fruits and vegetables were limited to Cuban oranges. In those days, most Ukrainians had only heard of bananas, pineapples, and coconuts. Today almost every possible tropical fruit and vegetable is available.

For the majority of Ukrainians, imported fruits and vegetables are not affordable. If you want to impress a Ukrainian, tell them that in your country bananas are cheaper than apples.

A fruit market in Kyiv.

However, visitors to Ukraine would be shocked at the prices of imported produce—at least twice the price on the world market. But when domestic fruits and vegetables are in season, they are "dirt cheap."

Because Ukraine's infrastructure is not developed enough to provide fresh produce all year round, seasonal canning is very popular. Jams, concentrated fruit drinks, tomatoes, cucumbers, and many other items are pickled or canned to be consumed in winter and spring, a vital necessity for most Ukrainian households. Every house and apartment complex is equipped with a cellar where jams and pickled vegetables are stored.

NATIONAL CUISINE

The best of East and West are combined in Ukrainian food. In general, the Ukrainian diet is fairly high in cholesterol, and the health conscious would probably look on it with disgust. However, compared to Central Asia, Ukrainian food is lean.

Ukrainians like spicy food, and tend to add more pepper, salt, and dill than German or British palates prefer. However, a Mexican or Korean would find the food mild. Ukrainians cook a variety of cutlets, hot cereals (including buckwheat, a grain which has almost been forgotten in the West), meat rolls, and milk products. Ukrainians are most famous for *borsch* ("BORSH"), known as "beet soup" abroad. But don't let the name disappoint you, because red beets are only one of the many ingredients that make up this delicious and nutritious soup.

Making pyrohy, dumplings filled meat, vegetables, or sweets.

Some of the other traditional Ukrainian dishes are *holubtsi* ("hoh-loob-TSIH"), rolls of cabbage, rice, and ground meat; *varenyki* ("vah-REH-nih-kih"), dumplings with fruit, potato, or meat filling; *deruny* ("deh-roo-NIH"), blintzes made of ground potatoes and flour; *pyrohy* ("pih-roh-HIH"), rolls with various fillings; and a variety of meat (mainly pork) products, especially cured meat. Ukrainians love *rybatska yushka* ("rih-BAHTS-kah YUSH-kah"), a fish soup that a skillful fisherman can make over an open fire.

While oysters, snails, or frog's legs are something many people in Ukraine would consider disgusting (though many others have never had the chance to try them), they do not hesitate to prepare beef or pork liver, tongue, lung paste, kidneys, brain, and even stewed bulls' tails, which are a rare delicacy. Hogs' trotters are widely used by cooks and homemakers to make jellied minced meat or aspic. Liver pie (ground liver mixed with fried onions and other ingredients, fried in the shape of pancakes, and arranged in layers) is also considered a delicacy to the Ukrainian palate.

Ukrainian kolach is a special bread made on festive occasions. Salt is sprinkled on top of the bread to celebrate the spice of life.

Each morning the "milk man" comes around to each farm house collecting milk.

DRINKS

Ukrainians do not drink much coffee, partly because it is not a traditional Ukrainian drink, but also because it is neither readily available nor affordable. Tea is greatly preferred, but iced tea is a strange concept to Ukrainians, who cannot imagine drinking tea any other way than hot. Juices, particularly apple, cherry, and apricot, are popular in the summer, as well as carbonated soft drinks and Russian *kvas* (fermented bread drink). Milk is drunk all year round.

ENTERTAINING AT HOME

The festive table is usually covered with a white embroidered tablecloth, crystal, and traditional decorations. The guests are seated in random order, although some reserve the ends of a rectangular table for special guests. Traditionally guests were seated so that no two men or two women were next to each other. Today, seating is more casual.

A Ukrainian table laid out for a meal.

ALCOHOL

Ninety-nine percent of festive dinners are served with alcohol. From time to time guests will propose a toast, usually to the health of the hosts, to friendship, and to prosperity. The procedure of drinking vodka at the festive table is different from many other cultures. Nobody drinks separately, and nobody sips their drink. The glasses are kept filled by the hosts at all times, unless the hosts designate someone else to the task.

Drinking beer from jars sold by street vendors.

UKRAINIAN HORILKA

A festive table in Ukraine is impossible to imagine without some kind of alcohol, particularly *horilka* (Ukrainian vodka), wine or, at the very least, beer. Horilka is rarely mixed in a cocktail, instead it is consumed as it is, without ice, in a portion of approximately two to four ounces. The only stipulation is that the bottle must be very well cooled in advance.

Alcohol has become a big social problem in Ukraine. Attempts to curb the consumption of alcohol have been largely unsuccessful. The most recent attempt to limit production and sale of horilka in favor of dry wines in 1985, known as "Gorbachev's Prohibition," resulted in a massive demolition of grape fields. In 1985, grape juice and wine production dropped significantly, but there was little or no impact on horilka production.

By law, people under the age of 21 are not permitted to buy alcohol, but in reality few salespeople pay attention to the age of the customer and are very rarely punished if caught.

A toast must be proposed before the glasses are emptied. When the toast is over, people usually clink their glasses (at least the first time) and drink—bottoms up! If and when someone starts "cheating" (that is, leaving some vodka in the glass), he or she is urged to finish the glass. It is close to impossible to refuse. However, unlike in Georgia or Armenia, it is not an insult to the host to refuse.

It is not unusual for each person to drink a half-liter bottle of vodka during a festive dinner.

Alcohol is also a very important part of Ukrainian hospitality. Social rules dictate that the hosts offer unlimited amounts of alcohol on special occasions. Visitors to Ukraine are not recommended to compete with Ukrainians in a drinking contest. One of the secrets of staying sober is to eat as much as possible in between toasts.

Beer and wine are also manufactured in Ukraine. Vineyards in the Crimea produce delicious dry wines, but these are generally not as popular as the traditional horilka and are rarely taken with meals, particularly festive meals. Beer is sold throughout Ukraine. Sometimes it is available on the streets drawn from large portable tanks.

Ukraine is not yet integrated into the system of world food distribution. Foreigners are unlikely to find many food or drink items so common in the rest of the world. Even Coke and Pepsi are not widely available.

Eating out at a café in Kyiv.

EATING OUT

Eating out in Ukraine is not nearly as popular as it is in some countries. Restaurant dining is very expensive, and the quality of food, on the whole, is not very good. More importantly, restaurants are not generally restricted to eating. Over the years, restaurants have become a place to go for a drink, rather than for a meal. Most Ukrainian waiters would be puzzled by an order of food and soft drinks, since it is better value to eat at home.

An accurate picture of most Ukrainian restaurants is loud music, singing, and cigarette smoke. However, recently, more and more private restaurants have opened to cater to a different sort of clientele.

Since Ukraine was a closed society for so many years, there are very few ethnic restaurants where one can try different varieties of regional foods. Ethnic food is still prepared primarily in the home, where, depending on the hosts background, one can be served Georgian *shashlyk* ("shahsh-LIK"), better known as shish-kebab in the West; Russian *pelmeni* ("pel-meh-nih"), meat dumplings; and Uzbek pilaf.

CHICKEN KYIV

4 boneless chicken breasts
$1/_4$ teaspoon salt
$1/_4$ teaspoon pepper
$1/_2$ cup butter
1 clove garlic, crushed
$1/_2$ cup chopped fresh parsley or 3 tablespoons dried parsley flakes
6 eggs
2 cups breadcrumbs
sunflower oil

Place each piece of meat between two pieces of waxed paper and beat with a hammer to flatten. Remove paper and sprinkle both sides of the meat with salt and pepper.

In a small bowl, mash butter with a fork and stir in garlic and parsley. Divide into four equal portions. Place a piece of meat on a flat surface. Place one portion of the butter mixture on the chicken breast's wider end. Fold each side over the butter and roll up the breast tightly. Do the same with the other three breasts.

In a shallow dish, beat eggs well. Pour breadcrumbs into another shallow dish. Dip a piece of chicken into eggs, coating thoroughly, then roll in breadcrumbs until completely covered. Repeat four times with the same piece of meat and set aside. Do the same with the other three breasts.

In a large frying pan, heat one inch oil (2.5 cm) over medium heat for 30 seconds. Carefully place chicken in pan with tongs and fry, turning frequently, until the meat turns a golden brown. Remove from pan with tongs and drain on paper towel. Just before serving, pierce each piece of chicken with a fork to let the butter run out.

Serves four.

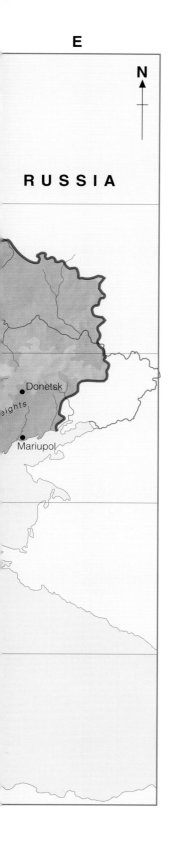

RUSSIA

Donetsk

eights

Mariupol

N

Azov Heights D3
Azov, Sea of D3

Belarus B1
Black Sea C5
Bulgaria A5

Carpathian Mountains A2
Cheremosh River A2
Chernihiv C1
Chernovtsy B3
Chornobyl C1
Crimea D4
Crimean Mountains D4

Danube River B4
Desna River C1
Dnipro River D3
Dnipropetrovsk D3
Dnister River B3
Donetsk E3

Hoverla, Mount A3
Hungary A3

Kakhovskoye D3
Kharkiv D2
Kherson C3
Kremenchugskoye C2
Kryvyy Rig D3
Kyiv C2

Lviv A2

Mariupol E3
Moldova B3

Nikolayev C3

Odesa C3

Poland A2
Poltava D2
Pripet Marshes B1
Privdennyy Bug River B2
Prut River B3
Pryp'yat River A1

Rivne B2
Romania A4
Russia E1

Sevastopol' D4
Slovakia A2
Stryy River A2
Symferopil D4

Turkey D5
Tysa River A3

Volhyn Uplands A2

Yalta D4

Zaporizhzhya D3

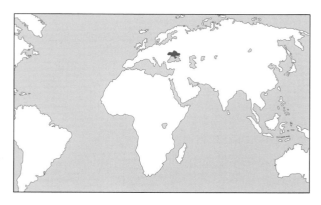

QUICK NOTES

OFFICIAL NAME
The Republic of Ukraine

LAND AREA
233,100 square miles (603,730 square km)

POPULATION
52.7 million

CAPITAL
Kyiv

NATIONAL SYMBOL
Trident

NATIONAL FLAG
Equal parts of blue (top) and yellow (bottom)

PROVINCES
Cherkasy, Chernihiv, Chernivtsi, Autonomous Republic of Crimea, Dnipropetrovsk, Donetsk, Ivano-Frankivsk, Kharkiv, Khmelnytskyy, Kyiv, Kirovohrad, Luhansk, Lviv, Mykolayiv, Odesa, Poltava, Rivne, Sumy, Ternopil, Transcarpathian, Vinnytsya, Volyn, Zaporizhzhya, Zhytomyr

MAJOR CITIES
Kyiv, Kharkiv, Odesa, Dnipropetrovsk, Lviv, Donetsk, Zaporizhzhya

HIGHEST MOUNTAIN
Mount Hoverla (6,751 feet/2,058 m)

MAJOR RIVERS
Dnipro, Dnister, Privdennyy Bug

NATIONAL LANGUAGE
Ukrainian

MAJOR RELIGIONS
Ukrainian Orthodox, Russian Orthodox, Greek Catholic

CURRENCY
hryvna

MAIN EXPORTS
Agricultural products, mineral fertilizers, steel

MAIN IMPORTS
Oil, natural gas, paper

IMPORTANT ANNIVERSARIES
Independence Day (August 24)
Victory Day (May 9)

POLITICAL LEADERS
Leonid Kravchuk, the first Ukrainian president after the Act of Independence of 1991
Leonid Kuchma, current president (1994-)

IMPORTANT LEADERS
Taras Shevchenko (1814–1861)
Bohdan Khmelnytskyy (1595–1657)
Ivan Mazepa (1639–1709)
Ivan Franko (1856–1916)
Lesya Ukrayinka (1871–1913)

GLOSSARY

bandura ("bahn-DOO-rah")
A multi-stringed, irregularly-shaped musical instrument.

bohomaz ("boh-hoh-MAHZ")
An artist specializing in religious design.

borsch ("BORSH")
A Ukrainian soup made with red beets, meat and many other ingredients.

chornozem ("chor-noh-ZEM")
Black soil.

hetman ("HET-mahn")
The title given to prominent Kozak leaders in the 15th–18th centuries.

hopak ("hoh-PAHK")
An energetic dance performed by men.

horilka ("hoh-RIL-kah")
Ukrainian vodka.

hryvna ("HRIV-nah")
The monetary unit in Kyivan Rus, reintroduced in 1996.

karbovanets ("kahr-BOH-vah-nets")
The temporary currency from 1992-1996.

kistka ("KIST-kah")
The tool used for drawing the wax pattern on Easter eggs.

kobzar ("kob-ZAHR")
A folk singer or bard.

Kozak ("koh-ZAHK")
A Ukrainian military man of the 15th–18th centuries.

krashanka ("KRAH-shahn-kah")
A Ukrainian Easter Egg, painted in one bright color.

Lavra ("LAH-vrah")
The monastery of the highest importance under the direct jurisdiction of the Patriarch of the Ukrainian Orthodox Church.

militsya ("mih-LIH-tsiah")
Police.

oblast ("OB-lahst")
State or province.

pyrohy ("pih-roh-HIH")
Rolls with various fillings, such as meat, vegetables, and sweets.

pysanka ("PIH-sahn-kah")
A Ukrainian Easter Egg with an artistic multi-colored design.

trembita ("trem-BEE-tah")
A wind instrument used in the Carpathian Mountains.

varenyki ("vah-REH-nih-kih")
Dumplings with various fillings.

BIBLIOGRAPHY

Farley, Marta Pisetska. *Festive Ukrainian Cooking*, Pittsburgh, Pa.: University of Pittsburgh Press, 1990.

Geography Department, Lerner Publications Company. *Ukraine*, Minneapolis, M: Lerner Publications, Co., 1993.

Hodges, Linda, and Chumak, George. *Ukraine: Hippocrene language and travel guide to*, New York, NY: Hippocrene Books, Inc., 1994.

Luciow, Johanna; Kmit, Ann; and Luciow, Loretta. *Eggs Beautiful. How to Make Ukrainian Easter Eggs*, Minneapolis, MN: Ukrainian Gift Shop, 1991.

Shevchenko, Taras. *Selected works, poetry and prose*, Moscow: Progress Publishers, 1979.

Shevchenko, Taras. *Taras Shevchenko, the poet of Ukraine; selected poems*, Jersey City, N.J: Ukrainian National Association, 1945.

INDEX

Aeroflot, 39
Afghanistan War, 107
agricultural output, 35, 41
alcohol, 119
Austria, 81
Azov Sea, 10, 11, 39, 102

Bachynskyy, Yulian, 21
Baiul, Oksana, 100
Baltic Sea, 18
Basil II, 17
BBC, 84
Belarus, 7
Black
    Sea, 7, 9, 10, 11, 13, 15, 18,
    39, 59, 102
Black Sea Shipping Company
    (BLASCO), 39
bohomaz, 89
Boiky. *See* minorities
borsch, 115
Bubka, Serhiy, 100

Bulgaria, 7, 18
Byzantine, 52, 74
Byzantine Empire, 72

Canada, 45
Carpathian
    Mountains, 8, 9, 10, 43,
    46, 47, 57, 93, 103
Central Asia, 18
Charles XII, 54
Cheremosh, 9
Cherkasy, 36, 74
Chernihiv, 43, 74
Chernyvtsi, 79
child-care, 62, 85
Chornobyl nuclear
    disaster, 25, 43, 69, 84
chornozem, 41
Christianity, 72–77
    architecture, 73, 74
    Catholicism, 75
    history of, 72

pre-Christian
beliefs, 71, 72, 77
restoration of, 71, 76,
    108
Churchill, Winston, 24
Cimmerians, 15
Committee for State
    Security, 28
Commonwealth of
    Independent States
    (CIS), 37, 100
Communism, 22, 76
Communist Party, 25, 29, 33
Constantinople, 72
Council of Ministers, 28
Crimea, 8, 10, 12, 16, 18,
    20, 48, 75
Crimean Mountains, 10
currency, 40
    hryvna, 40
    karbovanets, 40

INDEX

dance, 51, 94
hopak, 94
Danube River, 9, 18
Decembrists, 21
Department of
    Agriculture, 32
Desna, 9
diet, 113, 115
Dnipro River,
    8, 9, 13, 35, 39, 40, 103
Dnipropetrovsk, 8, 13
Dnister River, 9, 39, 103
Donetsk, 13
Dovzhenko, Oleksandr, 95

education, 63
egg decorating, 89, 91, 92
    krashanka, 91
    Petrykivka style, 92
    pysanka, 89, 91
embroidery, 50, 90
emigration, 45, 101
energy, 35, 43
    coal burning, 43
    hydroelectric power, 35,
    43
    nuclear power, 43
ethnic food, 120
exports, 37

famine of 1932-1933, 23, 113
farming
    collective, 23, 41, 42, 60
    private, 41, 42, 60
    state, 41
Fiodorov, Ivan, 87
First Crusade, 18
France, 7
Franko, Ivan, 95

Galicia-Volhynia, 18
Germany, 24
glasnost, 25
Golden Horde, 18
Gorbachev, Mikhail, 25
Greece, 52

horilka, 108
hospitality, 49, 117
housing, 58, 59
Hrushevskyy, Mykhailo, 22
Hulak-Artemovskyy,
    Semen, 95
humor, 52
Hungary, 7, 51
Hutsul, Tetiana, 100
Hutsuls. *See* minorities

icons, 89
immigration, 45
imports, 37
International Women's
    Day, 107
Islam, 48, 75

Judaism, 75

Karl XII, 20
KGB. *See* Commitee for State
    Security
Kharkiv, 13, 21, 39, 40, 95
Khazars, 17
Kherson, 9
Khmelnytskyy, Bohdan,
    20, 54
Kobzar, 55
kobzars, 92
kolach, 108, 116
Kotsubynskyy, Yuriy, 95
Kozaks, 13, 19, 20, 50, 74,
    77, 79
Kravchuk, Leonid, 25, 28
Kryvyy Rig, 40
Kuchma, Leonid, 25, 29
Kyi, Prince, 17
Kyrychenko, Raisa, 93
Kyiv, 8, 12, 15, 17, 21, 24, 40,
    69, 71, 72, 73, 74, 76, 83, 84,
    95, 98, 100, 106, 111
Kyiv University, 21
Kyivan Academy, 20
Kyivan

Rus, 17, 18, 71, 72, 73, 76
Kyivo-Pecherska Lavra, 17,
    76

Law on Television and Radio
    Broadcasting, 84
Lemky. *See* minorities
Lenin, Vladimir, 15, 22
Leontovych, Mykola, 93
literacy, 82
Lithuania, 18
Lviv, 7, 13, 24, 40, 58, 63,
    73, 81, 87, 89, 111
Lysenko, Mykola, 93, 95

manufacturing, 40
Mariinsky Palace, 27
Mariupol, 82
Matviyenko, Nina, 93
mass media, 79, 83, 98
Mazepa, Ivan, 20, 54
medicine, 64
military service, 31
Ministry of Environmental
    Protection, 28
Ministry of Home Affairs, 30
minorities, 45, 46-47
Misyutin, Hryhory, 100
Mohyla, Petro, 20
Moldova, 7, 18
Molotov-Ribbentrop Pact, 24
Mongols, 18, 54
Moscow, 20, 22
music, 92
Mykolayiv, 21

Nazis, 48
Nestor, 17
Novgorod, 73

Oblast Council of People's
    Deputies, 32
Oblast Executive
    Committee, 32
Odesa, 13, 21, 52, 53, 59, 71,
    77, 95, 100, 102, 111

INDEX

Oleg, Prince, 17

Parliament, 13, 25, 32, 61, 71, 79, 84. *See also* *Verkhovna Rada*
Paton, Yevhen, 40
patronymic names, 53
perestroika, 25
Pereyaslav Treaty, 20
Peter the Great, 21, 110
Petrenko, Viktor, 100
Petrograd, 22
Poland, 7, 18, 20, 51, 54, 81
Polovtsy, 18
Poltava, 20, 85
population, 45
    life expectancy, 69
private ownership, 27
privatization, 35, 36, 42, 67
Privdennyy Bug
    River, 7, 9, 39, 103
Pryp'yat, 9

Red Guards, 22
restaurants, 120
retirement, 62, 65
Rivne, 36, 43
Romania, 7, 9, 51
Romanovych, Danylo, 13
Romanovych, Lev, 13
Roosevelt, F. D., 24
Rukh, 25, 33
Rurik dynasty, 17
Russia, 7, 9, 20, 37, 45, 81
Russian
    Revolution, 22, 59, 76, 105

Sarmatians, 15
Savitskaya, Svetlana, 54
Scythians, 15, 16
Service for National
    Security, 28
Shevchenko, Taras, 55, 95
Siberia, 18, 48
Slavs, 13, 17, 18

Slovakia, 7
Smila, 40, 54
Solov'yanenko, Anatoliy, 93
sports, 99
St. Cyril, 81
St. Methodius, 81
St. Petersburg, 22
St. Sofia Cathedral, 89
Stalin, Joseph, 23, 24, 75
State Committee on
    Television and Radio
    Broadcasti, 84
Stryy River, 9
Symferopil, 40

Tatar Autonomous Soviet
    Socialist Republic
    (ASSR), 48
Tatars, 20, 48, 75, 87
    language, 87
tourism, 101
transportation, 39, 57, 68, 69, 100
Trypillians, 15, 89
Turkey, 7, 48
Turkmenistan, 37
Tysa River, 9

Ukrainian, 80, 81, 85, 86, 87
    Cyrillic alphabet, 81, 87
    dialects, 85
    relationship to
    English, 80, 86
Ukrainian Liberation
    Army, 107
Ukrainian Resistance
    Army, 24
Ukrayinka, Lesya, 54
unemployment, 38
Union of Soviet Socialist
    Republics (USSR), 7
United States, 45, 64
Ural River, 18
urban migration, 57

Verkhovna Rada, 27, 28, 31.
    See also Parliament
Victory Day, 107
Vikings, 17
Voice of America, 84
Volhynians. *See* minorities
Volodymyr,
    Prince, 17, 72, 73
Vovchok, Marko, 95

World War II, 24, 100, 106

Yalta, 15, 24, 37, 102
Yaroslav, Prince, 17
Young Communist
    League, 108

Zaporizhzhya, 40